# ALL MY PHLOX

# All My Phlox

## VALERIE STRONG

THE KENT STATE
UNIVERSITY PRESS
Kent, Ohio, & London

©1999 by The Kent State University Press,
Kent, Ohio 44242
ALL RIGHTS RESERVED
Library of Congress Catalog
Card Number 99-22302
ISBN 0-87338-634-5
Manufactured in China

05  04  03  02  01  00  99      5  4  3  2  1

Library of Congress
Cataloging-in-Publication Data
Strong, Valerie, 1926–
All my phlox / Valerie Strong.
p.    cm.
ISBN 0-87338-634-5 (cloth : alk. paper) ∞
1. Landscape architecture—Ohio Anecdotes.
2. Landscape
architects—Ohio Anecdotes.
I. Title.
SB470.54.O3S78      1999
712'.09771—dc21          99-22302

British Library Cataloging-in-Publication
data are available.

# Contents

Preface · vii

Acknowledgments · viii

1 Ohio · 1

2 Help! · 12

3 Connections · 24

4 The Barn · 37

5 Pools · 44

6 A Picnic · 56

7 August · 66

8 Turkey Manure · 77

9 By Committee · 88

10 The Secret Garden · 95

11 Forced · 103

12 Back to Ohio · 113

List of Plants

Mentioned in the Text · 120

# Preface

ALL WHO WORK with the land—homeowners, developers, farmers, and designers—are stewards of our most precious and yet most abused resource.

In particular, the landscape designer has a responsibility to set a course compatible with the urgent needs of the planet and to heighten awareness of physical and visual local conditions. A well-considered design will create a bond between man's contemporary manipulations and his surroundings—whether street, riverbank, or adjacent field. It is this spirit of place that is at the heart of environmental understanding. It is the spirit of place that will dictate the landscaping to us. Plants selected for tolerance to local conditions will thrive without the use of pesticides or irrigation and create an authenticity denied by exotics. This learning process begins by observing nature.

The homeowner has a unique opportunity not only to improve his own quality of life but also to monitor the activities of builders, contractors, and landscapers with whom he works. A good designer understands this and must be willing to assist the client in sharing with nature, in treading lightly on the land, in exerting true stewardship, in setting an example, in leaving even a small bit of the planet in felicitous harmony with nature. Together, client and designer become conservationists working together to understand one minute space, the better to stand against ignorance and greed.

# Acknowledgments

To HELEN, GEORGE, AND ROGER, who were ever ready to rescue me from overambitious projects.

Acknowledgments to Ohio, its subtle beauty and friendly people. Special thanks to all those professionals and clients, without whom there would have been no book.

Photography by Helen Strong, George Faddoul, and Valerie Strong.

# CHAPTER 1

# *Ohio*

Ohio is not a dramatic state—no mountains or ocean, just rolling hills, corn fields, woodlands, and Lake Erie, which is usually a dull pewter color. It is a state people say they have passed through—on the way to Chicago or New York, perhaps—but never itself a destination. But we do have the drama that comes with the seasons, spring and fall. Our autumn drama is obvious; brilliant leaf colors, berries, and golden fields bring the foliage pilgrims onto back roads to fill country inns and small-town squares. With spring all those intense colors of autumn—fiery red, burnished gold, and polished mahogany—are reborn as pastel lavender, pink, rose, and yellow, a landscape too subtle to draw the tourists.

What is not subtle is the intensity of Ohio spring. There is an inescapable vibrancy, a throb and excitement in every living thing, a hurry to nest, mate, sprout, or flower. The predawn rallying call of the cardinal outside my bedroom window seems to set off every bird in the neighborhood, newcomers and winter residents alike. How can I stay in bed with all that pulsing life outside—birdsong and the silent stirring of underground creatures and plants changing even by the day?

Within a block of my house I have about forty acres of "unimproved" land to walk in all weathers and seasons. I say "unimproved" because I can remember seeing these signs on vacant lots. Now the word of preference is "available," but in both cases it means that if you have the money you can cut, slash, bury, dump, or build—translated as lay waste—a developer's dream.

This rough landscape I have come to appreciate as much as any garden, especially as it is in such contrast to the surrounding perfect green playing fields of Western Reserve Academy, the private preparatory school here in Hudson, Ohio. This "unimproved" land, the playing fields, and the hockey pond at the bottom were once part of the Academy farm. The big dairy barn still stands at the edge of the fields, a historic reminder of a time when manual work was considered part of the educational curriculum and students helped with farm labor. Until about twenty years ago hay was cut here, so although the fields lay fallow, the second-growth woody plants are still tentative. We see a lot of these abandoned farm fields here in Ohio. Former farmland overgrown with shrubs, small trees, and "weeds" is great for developers, since the cost of cleaning out the "junk," as a client of mine persisted in calling any uncultivated land, is minimal.

The student cross-country track—and my walks—starts at the hockey pond, follows a rise to a hilltop planted in pines during a student tree-planting project, runs down through open meadow and on into another pine plantation, and then crisscrosses back up the hill to the hockey pond—a round of about a mile and a half. There is enough in these few acres to hold the interest of a student of nature for a lifetime, and this is where I meet Ohio's spring head on.

The buds of the red maples are in flower. The pussy willow catkins so soft a few days ago are already leaves, and here and there dandelions are blooming. A green fuzz has transformed the meadows, and the walk in the woods is like stepping into a pointillist painting, all soft dots of delicate color. The field paths are resilient underfoot, and my nose is tickled almost as much as my dog Amos's, but not for the same reasons. While he sticks to scenting out the passing rabbit or remains of an owl's dinner, the rank, damp smell of the earth awaking from its winter slumber fills and excites my senses.

From the first raucous call of redwings staking out nesting sites and robins gathering in the pines on their way north, the entire meadow takes on unstoppable momentum of growth and color and bloom—the woodies sprout new leaves, the grasses shoot up, clover stretches beside the path. Within weeks, it seems, there is the fragrance of thorn apples, the symbol of spring in abandoned Ohio farmlands, followed by the sweet

flowers of the wild locusts that edge the fields on one side, no doubt planted originally to serve as fence posts. The measured plumping of my tame buds at home is nothing compared to the exuberance of these fields in welcoming spring. And if a late snow or frost hits, the wild foliage doesn't need coddling with artificial covers; it simply closes, hiding like the rabbits until fair weather coaxes it out, unharmed, with every branch showing a new green. The multiflora rose, in dense tangles so beneficial to wildlife, will perfume the air in early summer as no fancy tea rose ever could. Blooming clusters of wild crabs are gathered like ballerinas in the wings, spring blossoms taking the summer to become the little red or yellow apples I pick for jelly in the autumn. The blackberries, too, are white with blossoms that become juicy fruit free for the picking. After the exuberance of spring, a quiet settling-in takes over the fields as the seasons unfold and ripen.

In even the few years I've been walking the fields, I've seen how quickly, once mowing stops, cultivated land reverts here in my part of Ohio to original hardwood forest. The meadow grasses give way to a tough mix of goldenrod, dock, milkweed, teasel, ironweed, daisies, black-eyed Susans, which are already being shaded out in places by sumac, gray dogwood, thorn apples, wild crabs, multiflora roses. If I live long enough, I'll be able to admire the next succession—oak, ash, maple, beech, hickory, tulip poplar—shade out the original woody plants. Without mowing there is no holding back this progression, where plants find their own habitat and bring with them their own wildlife. Without paying a cent, or levying new taxes, we have in our town a living laboratory.

Until the woodies take over, the fields are open enough for blackbirds to stake out nesting sites, rabbits to find cover, and hawks to follow both. We used to have bobolinks nesting, but their small corner was selected for "improvement" with early and close mowing. The bobolinks were a rare delight, like the English skylark, bursting with song while mounting straight up from the ground. Hearing them in the morning set the day right. If the mowing "fad" were outlawed, would the bobolinks return? I like to think so.

There are spectacular sights in these fields as well as the expected and commonplace. In summer, very early on a sunrise walk, if conditions are right, the whole field might be netted with spider webs, glistening in the new light. How can there be so many spiders? I examine the nets for the night's catch and find very little; perhaps it is already eaten. The webs are probably there every morning, but it is only on occasion that I have seen this fragile tenting of the fields, a sight to make anyone believe in fairies. In the very early morning, too, the paths are full of rabbits of every size, some just out of the nest. And it is also the early morning when the deer can be seen, though, unfortunately, this is not a wanted sight anymore.

No two days are ever the same on this walk. It can be as simple as the weather—lashing rain, lowering clouds, hot sun, humidity to cut with a knife—or as the change in foliage, the lengthening and heading out of various grasses, each with its own seed formation: timothy straight and tight, delicate lovegrass, downy bromegrass, and full-seeded fescue all intermingled with Queen Anne's lace, clover, hawkweed, daisies, black-eyed Susans, mustard, teasels, milkweed, lamb's quarters, dock, chicory.

This wild growth of the fields offers a perspective on our blink-of-an-eye life span, on our know-it-all monoculture landscaping. The pretty-faced upstarts in my garden cannot compare with these rugged field plants that have roamed the world for centuries to the benefit of man. What a wonder that the mullein, said to be the plant that Odysseus used to protect himself against the enchantress Circe, has settled in so happily at the gravel edge of the service road; or that chicory, which I admire for its unequaled blue flower, has been cultivated for four thousand years for the very same medicinal and culinary qualities it holds today. Without Queen Anne's lace, come to us most probably from Afghanistan, we might not have our modern carrot. The ferny-leaved yarrow took its name, Achillea, from the hero of the Trojan war, Achilles, who packed healing yarrow leaves on the wounds of his comrades. The stately milkweed is essential to the survival of the Monarch butterfly, which feeds in the caterpillar stage exclusively on this plant, taking in the toxins of the sap and nectar that stay with the adult butterfly as a unique predator control. And the burdock growing beside the historic barn should be remembered kindly for the long tradition of healing it has given to humanity. These wild plants that for centuries have been used for our health deserve better than the weed-eater from us now.

And what of today's children of weed-free suburbia, who are as deprived as children raised on city streets, deprived of feeling the prick of a thistle or teasel, of setting dandelion seeds afloat, of making a daisy chain, of sucking the sweet juice from a stem of grass? Are they destined to walk over sterile lawns and neat, mulched beds, never to pick a bouquet of wildflowers from a field or roadside?

5

⚓

Ohio

In autumn the fields turn ripe with goldenrod and wild asters and ironweed. Dock and teasel stand in rugged groups, and the milkweed cotton has scattered its rattling pods. Virginia creeper trails orange and red through dead elm and wood edge. Berries hang from every shrub—the fox grapes, the multiflora rose, serviceberry, gray dogwood, and (if you can call them berries) the chartreuse osage oranges.

There are winter sunrises, when the low sun lays down a wash of palest pink over untracked snow. The hockey pond in winter lives up to its name when children clear the ice for skating and novice skiers practice on the gentle runs of the summer cross-country course.

Winter is the time to find out who lives here and there, to walk the fields and pine stands to study the tracks. There are snow-burrow runs of voles that cross the path to disappear suddenly and for no apparent reason. The fox's night prowl can be tracked, and the rabbit's dinner evaluated, at the base of the crab apples. The old osage orange trees, once planted in a line, as fences, have long since dropped their huge pomanders (I'm told they sell in New York as roach deterrents), which now lie shredded by rabbits and squirrels. And there are other life-and-death struggles: the feathers of an unfortunate bird, a frozen vole, bits of fur left by a hawk, owl, or fox.

All this abundance and diversification takes place without human intervention. The shrubs, trees, and grasses grow and die without planting or harvesting. The animal and bird life they shelter emphasize, in a shrinking natural world, the value of a few acres *not* set aside as a park or bike trail or golf course but of "unimproved" land. If we can appreciate these few acres, if they can be left alone, then there is hope that we shall preserve the grander spaces of our planet.

Hudson, where all this takes place, the town where I live and work, is a Western Reserve town founded in 1779 by Connecticut pioneer David Hudson. The Connecticut Western Reserve was land set aside for settlement by Connecticut families in a 120-mile band roughly from the Pennsylvania border as far west as Norwalk, Ohio. These original settlers' houses, Greek Revival or Federal in style, still stand throughout the villages and farms of northern Ohio and are the backbone of the landscape. Towns were usually built around a central green with the church as the first communal building constructed. Here in Hudson there is a remarkable number of these Western Reserve houses, and we have the added bonus of the Western Reserve Academy, originally a college and now a private preparatory school. The first teachers, Yale graduates, built the Academy's "Brick Row" modeled on that of Yale. It is an impressive walk, with the chapel, built in 1836; the president's house, built as a double house in 1829 in Federal style; North Hall, built as a dormitory in 1837; Seymour Hall, built in 1913 to replace original buildings lost to fire; and the Loomis Observatory, erected in 1838.

When involved with landscaping in Hudson, or anywhere, for that matter, the history and style of house dictates what is possible. Here, even with considerations for modern living, the nineteenth-century atmosphere is achieved mostly through restraint. It is difficult to tell people who have the money to "fix up the place" that sometimes doing nothing is best.

One of my first volunteer jobs was planning a garden for the 1835 Morley Cottage used by Western Reserve Academy as a faculty residence. In part it was done to appease a new headmaster who found Brick Row too bare. His eye was unaccustomed to the lack of foundation plantings or flower beds; to him it seemed stark. My suggestion was to retain this authentic simplicity and add a garden around the old house, where a garden belonged. Landscaping falls to fashion as does everything else, and it is hard not to succumb to what we see around us, especially if we have no historical perspective. In today's style, buildings cannot stand alone; foundation plantings are a must, inappropriate though they might be for nineteenth-century buildings. Plantings are piled up until the all-too-familiar, generic landscaping of the country club and mall are in place.

The best way to develop a feel for the nineteenth-century atmosphere is to look at old photographs of the days before lawn companies and weed-eaters, which have cursed us only since the 1950s. There one sees a simplicity that cannot be missed. Often the grass has rough edges, a weed shows against a tree or foundation, deciduous shrubs arch at the corners of the houses, schools and churches stand in grass sheltered by a few stately trees. It is difficult for our modern eye to readjust to this simpler way, and so much is available today that it's difficult to resist the impulse to buy an unrelated confusion of plants that would not even make a good botanical garden.

For Morley Cottage, in a visible position on the Academy campus, it was decided to create a garden that would reflect the date of the house and the history of the village, thus putting the garden where it belonged so that the beautiful buildings of Brick Row could be left in their classic simplicity.

The first step was to tear out the taxus, those ubiquitous shrubs of the 1940s and 1950s. (Today they have been superseded by gold-thread juniper, purple plums, and rhododendron, no matter what the soil or exposure.) A picket fence was installed along the walk to the side of the property to tie into an existing hedge across the front. An arbor covered the walk to the rear door, and brick walks defined the new vegetable plots. The entire side garden was filled with cottage garden flowers, with particular emphasis on spring and autumn blooms, when the students are on campus. The final result was breathtaking. Apothecary roses hung over the pickets, New Dawn covered the opening to the arbor, and grapes soon took over the rest of it. The rose, Louise Odier, was planted in the front of the house to offer fragrance to those walking in or out. The artemisias, nepeta, borage, thyme, sidalcea, hollyhocks, achillea, allium, cosmos, cleome, heliotrope, nicotiana, among others, created a profusion of bloom. Along the rear fence asparagus, rhubarb, and strawberries were planted. The whole atmosphere was that of a garden appropriate to the period, and indeed this effort won the county's historic landscape award.

This success would be nothing today if not for Lynna. I had learned the hard way that planting the garden is only the first step—it must also be maintained. My volunteer efforts for the Academy were too limited. What they needed I emphasized, was a full-time person who knew what he or she was doing, especially someone who knew how to prune. (This is an art very few understand.) The deciduous shrubs of the campus had gone untended or been chopped at random when branches encroached on a path, and the hedges that now replaced the wood fences enclosing the original campus were no more than nubby twigs.

It was Lynna who answered the ad placed in the local paper, and by chance I happened upon her as she was looking for the office for an interview. Radiant as an Irish beauty, her smile, her laugh, her quick wit, her love of the outdoors and plants won me over instantly. We took a walk, long enough for me to find out that she was a trained horticulturist and that she not only knew how to prune but loved doing it. "It's my therapy," she told me.

Since then, she has become not only a good friend but an invaluable colleague. Here is someone to talk shop with; to study catalogs with over lunch; to exchange ideas, cuttings, seeds, frustrations, successes. She comes into the house like a ray of sunshine—such a trite expression except when describing Lynna. She has the ability to lift spirits, to make us laugh, and her optimism is unfailing. How did we ever get along without her?

And the pruning? It took her three years to make the first round, rejuvenating the hedges and all the shrubs by cutting old growth to the ground—as should be done. But now the spirea arches gracefully, the mock orange is white with fragrant blooms, and the once-struggling lilacs have shown their appreciation by bursting with flowers. Best of all, Lynna has an appreciation for the history of the campus and town. She spent hours in the Academy and town archives and dug up photographs and papers about the landscaping. She knows every tree. She knows when changes were made, when the faculty garden was constructed, and all the stories surrounding it. She has a sense of appropriateness for the campus, a sense of the spirit of place. As long as Lynna is in charge, we can all rest assured that the campus is in good hands. It won't look slick!

When I started my career as a landscape designer, along with volunteer and local jobs, I was working at accumulating credentials, starting with design courses offered by Ohio State University. I loved it all. I read, attended every seminar I could, and haunted the Lake County nurseries, the most extensive in the country, to study plants in the field. As soon as I was able, I took off to England for courses there and to France to visit gardens and take notes and photographs. Later, when my career was well under way, I attended the La Napoule Landscape design courses, where I was very much influenced by English designer John Brookes and the American Jim Van Sweden.

Later, in Holland, I discovered the intimate gardens of Mien Ruys, gardens like Vermeer paintings. It was like a seminar to sit in her "example" gardens and study her hardscape and layering of plants, the foliage, the way she achieved intimacy, her attention to detail. I was lucky, too, to be able to walk the gardens with her and listen to her comments about what she had done and why and to learn that her garden philosophy was so in tune with my own.

But it wasn't as if I knew nothing about plants and soil going into this; I had been pottering around in gardens all my life, wherever I lived. It's impossible not to learn what grows in sun or shade, how to enrich the soil, when to plant, how to divide—all the minutiae of gardening that, like cooking, come through trial and error and observation.

Sweet peas, so glorious in Wisconsin, burned out in Ohio. I gave up trying to reproduce the giant rhododendrons of Belgium and learned that the lavender that covers the mountainsides of Greece cannot be relied on in our severe winters, any more than the annual combination seen in England of geraniums and lobelia can be counted on to survive the heat of our summers. I learned the hard way that it is folly to try to create an English garden in the Midwest extremes of heat and cold. I learned the importance of, what might be called in art, negative space, the empty space, and the importance of scale and the framed view to avoid "visual indigestion." I came to understand the human desire to control nature and my own reaction against this desire in our controlled times.

College art history courses, all those lessons in perspective and balance and symmetry, took on new meaning when I studied the green Italian gardens with fountains and views to the distance. The same could be said for my sympathy for the Islamic garden with its water and quartered beds, a design handed down to us until the English "natural" garden movement.

I learned the meaning of garden "paradise" from living in, visiting, or hiking in dry climates like Greece, Jordan, Cyprus, Eastern Turkey, Egypt, and Iran. I felt the relief green gives the eye, the soothing influence of water, the languid effect of fragrance, and the utter contentment of relaxing in a garden space. I came in from the desert to just such a garden as is depicted in the miniatures. The relief to my senses, which closed down in desert heat like the eyes and nostrils of the camel, was an almost mystical experience, a spiritual nourishment. How can I forget the fragrance of roses and jasmine and stocks, the rest for the eye that no artifice such as sunglasses can equal; the sound of water when one's lips are cracked from thirst; the repose in shade—the luxury of shade? This is garden. This is Eden.

It is this vision of Eden that has haunted me through the years and that I now try to create for my clients in our own context of high-pressure lives and exuberant vegetation.

It was all this lifetime of seeing where plants grow naturally and looking at so-called weeds and the symbiosis of plants everywhere I went, from English hedgerows to the monastery courtyards of Cyprus and Greece, that has made me appreciate what grows naturally anywhere. The rock defiles of Petra are graced with trailers of caper plants or wild oleanders. In Cyprus spring transforms the moonscape to a millefleurs carpet. In Greece what we consider garden plants—iris, peony, gladiolus, anemones, cyclamen, poppies—cover the springtime mountains. The wild vegetation emphasizes the "spirit of place" that is so often defied in our landscape attempts. By observing nature it is possible to come to an understanding of what looks "right"—a vague term, like clothes that suit one person and not another. It was an effort to synthesize these collected experiences, feelings, and convictions that drove me on to become a landscape designer right here in Ohio.

# CHAPTER 2

# *Help!*

Must like hard outdoor work, all weather. Full or part time, flexible hours. Installation and maintenance of perennials and landscape plants. Will train.

Τ HIS WAS MY AD. It was February, which here in Ohio can be a depressing month, the sleet and cold only to be survived by thoughts of spring flowers. But my thoughts turned to wheelbarrows, digging forks, manure, and incessant hard work. I should have felt elated that my business as a landscape designer, which I had started late in life, only two years previously, had taken off with wild success. The fact was that it had become too much for one person—that person being me—and I couldn't see my way out of it.

What had happened was that the gardens I had installed now needed maintenance. What most people didn't realize, and I had not emphasized enough, was that perennial beds require very high maintenance, and herb gardens even more. A client called last autumn to tell me in an accusing tone, as if it were my fault, that her dooryard garden was a mess and her husband was complaining. "He's a neatnick," was her description of him. "And after all the money I spent," she went on, "the yard doesn't look anything like the pictures I showed you." We both learned a lesson. She, that you can't disappear to the cottage in July and August and expect to return to a gorgeous garden unless someone has been on hand to weed and water. I, that I must not only stress maintenance but be able to provide it.

Maintenance was what I was thinking about now during the February thaw, wondering how I was going to spread all the needed manure and do all the digging and pruning as well as the planning, ordering, consultations, potting the containers, and finding some of the more unusual plants, not to mention the billing. With this mental list I froze. Not even the seed catalogs, my usual remedy for February doldrums, could cheer me. I avoided planning and ordering by fussing around the house tidying drawers and mopping the kitchen floor (always low priority with me), feeling more and more depressed about the work I should be doing and wasn't. My disposition gave out, and to keep from being totally obnoxious I retreated to my room with a book—not even a garden book but a Judge Dee murder mystery.

"I don't know why you don't get someone to help you?" My youngest daughter, Helen, asked practically as she chopped vegetables for a stir fry. She is a free-lance photographer with a studio over the garage and a penchant for cooking.

I pushed another log into the wood stove and hung over its heat. "Who would I get? How many people are there who know anything about gardens. I can see it now all the flowers pulled out and the weeds left."

"You could teach them. Just put an ad in the paper. There is bound to be some crackpot who doesn't mind being miserable all the time."

Helen had been pressed into service on various critical occasions—"critical" meaning when it was too cold, wet, or muddy for me to find anyone else willing to work.

"Everything you do is so difficult—heavy or hard—and the weather is always awful when you do it." She much preferred to do her work from behind the lens of a camera.

But her suggestion was so simple I wondered why it hadn't occurred to me. Looking back, I think that the whole garden design business had expanded so fast that I never envisioned more than I could manage alone, and I could not foresee expansion because I still felt so tentative myself.

Hence the ad in the local paper. At least, I thought, only the serious would answer an ad like that, especially given the hard work part. Probably there would be no answers. Now that the ad was in, I realized that it was unrealistic to think that in this age of soft living I would find anyone willing to plant bulbs in snow, prune through tangled shrubs including barberry and roses, spread manure by the wheelbarrow load, and tend plants in ninety-degree heat. No, I moaned, the chances of finding in the same person a plant and nature lover, physical strength, *and* willingness were nil. I prepared myself to sit beside a silent phone and became more depressed than ever.

The first of the calls came about tea time the day the ad came out, and they didn't stop coming for three days. Helen couldn't believe that there were so many out there who said they liked hard work. Moving away from my go-it-alone mentality, I jumped in one bound to visions of all that I could do with armies of men and women who were willing to go forth into sleet, snow, rain, and heat to dig, shovel, and scratch. I took down names and telephone numbers in my notebook; the list grew to twenty-three applicants, all of whom assured me over the phone that they loved hard outdoor work.

But it was Kristine who came for an interview the very first evening. She was stunningly beautiful. Untamed long brown hair framed her face. Her eyes danced with health, humor, and good nature, and she had an assurance that I knew instinctively was from her own serenity. And there was about her an aura, an inner glow, which later I found shone out of her philosophy of life and the discipline of meditation. We discussed the work to be done; when I mentioned the need to spread manure, she never flinched.

"Then you don't mind a dirty job like that, or pushing heavy wheelbarrows?"

"This is the very job I'm looking for, where I can work with Mother Earth using organic methods."

I explained that I continued to garden for others as I had for myself for thirty years, never using sprays or pesticides but replenishing the soil with organic matter to make healthy and therefore disease-resistant plants.

"When would you like me to start?"

The promise of shoveling manure seemed to be an enticement. It couldn't be possible. Here was the goddess Rhea herself offering to slog for me. We hadn't even discussed the practicalities of wages, hours, clothes, location of jobs, and transportation. But there were no problems. Everything seemed ideal. Kristine already had a part-time job, but she could arrange her hours to suit mine. And so it was

that Kristine came into our lives. I say "our" because she was such a force for good that she affected all of us.

"You've lucked out," Helen, who had joined the last few minutes of the interview, said when Kristine left. "What a knockout!"

And I couldn't believe my luck. We had decided before Kristine left that we would tackle the manure spreading in two days—weather permitting.

That was settled, but I still needed someone else.

Then Nancy called. She lived nearby, wanted part-time work, but with grown children the hours could be steady when the push was on and planting couldn't be delayed. Her former job had been with a bank, and she'd had it with indoor work. She didn't care what the job was or how hard as long as it was outdoors. In fact, what surprised me about the applicants I couldn't hire—despite my fantasy of sending out scores of workers each day to beautify the world—was their sincerity about loving outdoor labor. It was comforting to know that not everyone wants to dress up to work in an office under fluorescent lights.

Nancy was quiet, capable, steady, practical, and very intuitive. She and Kristine became soul mates. Nancy sympathized with Kristine's mental and physical health precepts, and as we worked together over the years, if we were not converted, we were both in awe of Kristine's discipline.

It was the beginning of a five-year relationship with working partners that I think is seldom attained. This is the way we worked. We would discuss the possible jobs for the following day; but as weather is such a determining factor, there were confirmation calls in the morning. I might go on a pickup with an agreement to meet them on the job with the plants. While waiting for me, they would be pruning, digging, edging, or doing any other work that needed to be done. Or we might go all together (some jobs were over an hour's drive), the van loaded with tools, usually some plants, and, in those years, Amos, my standard poodle. In some cases there were several jobs in the same area, which meant a varied day, as they all had differing requirements.

The three of us worked smoothly with no orders given or plans prearranged. I couldn't help but wonder if it weren't because we were women that we could work so independently. At the job we would fan out, each taking on a separate task according to our own likes or priorities. Nancy loved weeding and could not walk past any bed without a swipe from her Smith and Hawken weeder. Kristine and I liked the tougher things, like pruning, transplanting, working in compost or manure. Nancy was the clean-up person—a job I hate. As Kristine and I flung prunings and snippings, they would vanish into Nancy's bag; she would empty our buckets and always sweep so that no traces of how we worked could be seen on terrace, lawn, or walk. It was wonderful, smooth and efficient. We each saw the work that needed doing and moved in on it without discussion or argument.

None of us was into regular breaks. Usually we worked until thirst or hunger dictated a pause—and that is all it was—before we started in again. But as the day wore on and we wore out, having accomplished more than any workers I've ever known, we might take half an hour to stretch in sun or shade, depending on the weather, to listen to the birds and enjoy the properties as the owners, with their high-pressure careers, seldom could.

Our jobs were anywhere within an hour and a half from home and were of all sizes, from large estates and commercial properties to intimate town gardens. For clients farther afield, I trained the local gardener or supervised the construction and installation.

There were places where the atmosphere was so serene and the silence so profound that the snip of the Felco pruners seemed loud. These were the gardens from which we left at the end of the day tired, but not irritated. It was the clients and their attitude toward nature, as much as the surroundings, who created what I with plans or we with rakes and hoes could never accomplish alone. What a difference it made if the owner came out to warn us of a bird's nest while we were pruning or led us through the woods to a mellow compost heap or, like the owner of the tiny city garden, took time to tell us the stories behind the sculptures and works of art or ask how we could bring in more birds and butterflies. These properties seemed to have a life of their own.

There were other properties that made all of us uneasy, especially Nancy (who would be intent on nose-to-ground weeding), when the client came out, looking more prickly than any thistle, to discuss progress or, more likely, to complain.

"Real bad vibes here," she would say. She was always right. These were the places where the housewife was tense, nervous, and aggressive, and the gardens were not for pleasure but for show—a show of money—and these women were cutthroat about producing a garden that would best those of neighbors. The properties were possessed by virtue of money, and any vegetation that had not been bought and paid for was ruthlessly rooted out as being unworthy. And woe to me if any of the bought-and-paid-for died, even though I explained repeatedly that plants do die.

Ten years ago these same people would have put a pot of geraniums on the front step and called it summer; but now Americans have discovered gardens, and no one can be without one, even if it goes against their nature, as well as *Mother* Nature.

There was the client who apologized when we looked over the new house surrounded by clay to the fringe of woods to the rear.

"I know it looks messy," she said, "but it's been too wet for the bulldozer to get in." It took me an instant to realize that it was not the recently graded clay she was referring to but the remnants of the original wooded lot. I pointed out that the mess of trees was the only mitigating asset on a desecrated property.

"Oh no, we want to plant pine trees so there will be something green in winter. All that stuff," she looked at me wide eyed, almost with innocence, "will turn brown, then all winter there's nothing to look at."

In these circumstances I try to convert. I pointed out that what she and her husband considered nothing was indeed a remnant of magnificent Ohio mixed-hardwood forest. I took her back, through oozing clay, to point out the wild cherry, maples, hickory, ash. At the edge I found some sassafras and crushed the leaves for her to smell and showed her the three shapes; the palm, the thumb and the finger and told her that even if she ached for a sassafras and was willing to pay for it, she couldn't have one, because they are so difficult to transplant, and I didn't know of anyone growing them commercially—but here she had this rarity, God given. (It always helped to have God on my side.) After all, anyone can have a pine tree.

The woods stayed.

There was the client who called from her car phone to tell me that Mikey wanted a perennial that would flower all summer to grow under the pines and spruce.

"You know the place," she said. "Where it is nothing but pine needles and all brown. Mikey wants color there, maybe red."

To this one I answered that as soon as God created such a miraculous plant—a red perennial that would grow and bloom all summer in dense shade, in a mat of pine needles—Mikey would be the first to know.

Or the client who told me that she couldn't sleep at night thinking about the moles eating her plants. I was supposed to produce some lethal mole poison instead of telling her how fortunate she was that in this troubled world this was the only problem that disturbed her sleep.

Often on such jobs, to keep our sanity we would redesign house, garden, and people. Our quick-fix method was to bomb the house and start over or, if the house was not too tasteless and pretentious, make it disappear under vines or, as landscape architects have done for years, in a forest of trees.

At the height of our reeducation plans for the owners, the pruners snipped at a furious rate, and every new plan—like our fantasy correctional institutions in Maine, where there are no facilities, no running water, wood stoves, outdoor plumbing, no air conditioning, and no cars—sent us into a frenzy of work.

"Can you see those heels out hauling water?"

"What about the makeup? We have to ban mirrors."

"What about getting along with the neighbors?"

"They never could—not with Mainers."

Pickups in the spring were constant and exhausting. Before I even went to the nursery, I'd stake where each plant was to go, and we'd try to have the holes dug ahead and have water available. At the nursery I had loading help, but when I arrived at the job with an overload of trees and shrubs, then it was only we three to get these bagged and burlapped plants out of the van and into the wheelbarrow, with Kristine always on the heavy end, never even questioning that anything was beyond our strength. This was when the joy of planting ceased to thrill and became no more than an endurance contest. Together we did a tremendous amount of heavy labor. Planting perennials was just as difficult as planting shrubs, because I insisted that the perennial beds be adequately prepared with quantities of humus or manure and deep tilling. The pickax was our indispensable tool for tree planting, and we would take turns at hacking the huge holes, often into rock or clay. The time came, however, when even *we* three needed help.

There was a big job coming up. It had been fun in the planning because Ernie, the property owner, and I were in accord from the first. He wanted less lawn, an end to mowing a steep bank, and a feature made of the shale outcrop on one side of the lot. He loved the woods coming almost to the back door and all the creatures associated with it. He was fed up with the minimal plantings of taxus that the developer had given him and with working against nature.

The house was on a new street that had been cut into a shale outcrop through beautiful hardwood forest. Unfortunately, as is so frequently the case, the builder had never considered where he was building. It should have been a street of natural wonder and architectural creativity, with tucked-in houses clinging to rock or overhung with trees. But the rocks had been blasted or cleared, and pretension found an outlet in a ragout of styles where the only criterion was big. This one street had it all: the so-called Palladian windows, vast enough to show off the brass and glass chandeliers dangling in the "cathedral" foyer; multimedia entrance pillars to drives lined with lights suitable for a freeway intersection. With all signs of natural vegetation removed, ownership was shown in expensive "landscaping," all dependent on life-support systems. How can the miserable blue spruce and purple plums replace the original beech-hickory-maple-ash forest? But bought and paid for (money, money, money) are the rhododendrons in front of south-facing brick walls and enormous trees hauled in at great expense to stand isolated and suffering in chemically treated lawn.

Ernie's house was unlike all the others. He had no hint of pretension. "I think the developer ran out of money when he got this far down the street," Ernie told me. "What I don't want is that." He pointed next door.

Despite his sensitivity to the natural surroundings, Ernie was too gentle and nonconfrontational to go along with my half-serious suggestion to let the straggly lawn go its own way. It was a relief to him then when he saw my plan, which would keep the homeowner's association from suing for neglect but still satisfy his longing for and my insistence on a blend with nature.

I recommended for on the bank fading into the woods understory trees—serviceberry, hawthorn, witch hazel, viburnum, Cornelian cherry, bayberry—to give the effect of a natural copse. Near the street mugho pines, a few ornamental grasses, daylilies, and sedums made it more gardenlike. It was to be the kind of planting that in three years would look as if it had evolved on its own. There were to be later additions of herbs and a few flowers around the door, but we both agreed that the rock outcrop should be preserved in its skeletal outline.

Then came the planting. Unfortunately, Nancy couldn't work on this job, but Kristine volunteered Gregory, the male equivalent of Kristine herself. A nature photographer, he was good looking in a rugged, lean, outdoor way, about six-two, very easygoing but deep. He was a lover of nature and an adventurer in it. He and Kristine would go out West every chance they got, doing all sorts of daring athletic things, like rock climbing, skiing, and hiking in wilderness areas.

But we needed still another man. So Bill arrived—a mountain man, with his own pickup, wanting a summer job. Heavy-set, bearded, and strong, Bill was a graduate engineer who wanted to make enough money doing summer work outdoors to drive out West. One look at him and his truck and he was hired. As it turned out, we all lost our hearts to him. Here was the macho male in spades who had no qualms about working with three women; he was unfailingly thoughtful, volunteering for long hours, pickups, pickax duty, lifting, hauling, anything. And did we need him! It is amazing how people turn up just when they are most needed.

Kristine and I planned Ernie's planting job as if we were entering an Outward Bound program. What we hadn't planned for was the unpredictable Ohio climate—this time heat. Who would expect the temperatures to be in the nineties in May?

Bill in his truck and I in my van, we did the plant pickup the day before as scheduled. We were delayed for hours at the nursery, which was in the midst of the usual spring frenzy, and the plants were much heavier than we had expected, so the unloading was a struggle with no front-end loader. Even Bill thought he'd had a workout by the time the plants were dropped off in Ernie's drive and watered in. But it was nothing compared to the exhaustion we felt at the end of the following day.

I had gathered lengths of hose to soak and spray the plants. Gregory brought his own pickax. I provided two wheelbarrows, tarp, and all the usual shovels and rakes, as well as lots of water bottles and lemons. We decided to start at 6:00 A.M. so that we could have the job finished before the afternoon sun laid us low. What a joke!

It was a slope we were planting. We had three one-inch hawthorn, four six-foot serviceberry, four five-foot witch hazel, three four-foot bayberry, three four-foot blackhaw viburnum, five four-foot burkwood viburnum for fragrance, three juniper, one five-foot cornelian cherry, and three mugho for the front around rocks, and of course the ornamental grasses, five reed grass and ten little blue stem.

With the first test shovel I groaned. Rock! What else could there be with shale outcroppings all around us? We didn't dig. We mined. The men used picks with powerful overhead swings that, even watching, jarred my arm when they struck. Thinking of Helen, and her complaints about my jobs, I asked Gregory how he could stand this kind of work when he could be behind the lens of a camera. He straightened to his lean height and said matter of factly that it was no worse than splitting wood.

We worked with desultory conversation, a few jokes about the heat, the thorns, the digging. The men paused every so often to compare notes on other life-threatening experiences they had survived. Planting for Ernie seemed to be right up there with the time Greg lost his way hiking in a canyon in Utah with only one water bottle. For Bill it was a winter he spent in a cabin in Maine. The ax replaced the pick he held now, but the pull on the back muscles was the same, Bill assured us.

It was too early for cicadas, but it was that same kind of heat, the kind that made you want to lie around with lemonade and listen to them sing. Humid, still, languid. The air was so heavy it seemed visible, like working in a fog. It became another force to fight against. Voices were muffled. The only smart one was Amos, who had stretched out into moist soil he had dug from a groundhog hole.

I, in the meantime, felt total guilt. It was my bad judgment that we were all paying for. How could I expect anyone to do this kind of work with no machinery? I suggested a jackhammer. Too much noise, the men said. At one point Greg straightened, wiped the sweat from his forehead with a muddy arm, and, grinning, said that this was like trailblazing out West. "Just different scenery when you come up for air." We looked across the street to the chem-green lawn surrounding an institution-sized house of unbelievable ugliness—such a contrast to our vision of Western trails. We all laughed. It was only the jokes and laughter that eased the strain enough to get us through the day.

By the time every plant had a new home and I could see the end in sight, a cool evening breeze had come up, and I set off for a twelve-pack.

Sprawled on the grass, brew in hand, Bill wondered how anything could grow in such conditions. This was a thought I had been keeping to myself all day. I had reasoned that there had been woods here originally, so why wouldn't these new plants love the free root run? Kristine, as she watered in each plant before we left, talked to them and stroked the stems.

"They'll grow," she said.

This became the job by which all others were judged—they were as bad or not nearly as bad or almost as bad as planting at Ernie's. But it was the help that made it possible.

And did the plants survive? Beautifully! Six years later, the growth is full, with all season interest from the very early blooms of the serviceberry in spring to bright autumn foliage, from the winter berries of bayberry, hawthorn, and viburnums to the changing grace of the ornamental grasses. We learned that most plants will do better even on rock than in heavy clay.

And what about talking to them? Kristine says the proof is there to see.

# CHAPTER 3

# *Connections*

ONE OF THE MOST unexpected perks of my job has been meeting people I would otherwise never have met. I've made contacts and friendships everywhere—clients, of course, of all types, but also nurserymen, plant breeders and horticulturists, construction workers, stone masons, landscapers, designers and landscape architects, carpenters, and all those on the "low end" who load, heave, fetch, or dig. All have made my life richer. But the nursery people, from one-man operations like Horace Wilson's to the huge complex at Lake County Nurseries, have made it possible for me to do quality work, thanks to the design selection and the superior grade of plants available to me.

Along the southern shore of Lake Erie, from Mentor to Madison, lie some of the largest nurseries in the world. They benefit from the sandy soil of the ancient lake bed and the climate moderated by proximity to the Great Lake Erie. Even an hour's drive south to Hudson, where I live, the climate is harsher, colder in winter and hotter in summer.

For anyone interested in plants, Lake County, Ohio, is paradise. For me it has been both laboratory and graduate school, my professors being the growers, propagators, and others who work with plants I would only be able to read about but never see in the field. Plant people are incredibly generous with their time and knowledge and are willing, even from a phone call, to offer advice.

In spring, when the rush is on, I might have to pick up orders at four different nurseries in one day. If I need ground covers—maybe partridgeberry, which is difficult to find, or the unusual 'Dart's Golden' ninebark or the common lemon lily, which used to be found in every farmyard and has languished in favor of larger cousins and which I find indispensable for old-fashioned gardens—then my first stop would be at Kingwood.

I usually leave extra early to go there, not because it is so far away (although it is the farthest), but because I treat myself to a detour through the town of Madison, which is a treasure of Western Reserve houses. Madison has not expanded so much that the intimacy of the nineteenth century has been lost, and certainly anyone interested in scale and proportion, which I find the most difficult aspects of design, can do well to study these early Ohio houses—their relationship to the surroundings, the wings as they relate to the main structure, the scale of windows, doors, and ornamentation. It is a relief, too, after seeing so many of out-of-scale, pretentious houses in current fashion, to come back to the simple elegance of a Greek Revival facade.

If I have any bonus time at all, I drive the extra miles to Unionville to look at Shandy Hall, one of the oldest houses in the Western Reserve, with the original portion dating to 1815. It is hard to relate the struggles of those early days to the tamed countryside of today with its nurseries, farms, and vineyards.

The office at Kingwood Nursery is comfortingly tucked in the rear of a tree-protected Western Reserve farmhouse. No matter how busy they are, staff members have time for greetings and talk, which invariably includes the weather.

I might go next to Losely, where perhaps on a previous visit I had found some good-sized common lilacs or tagged some deciduous holly. In the yard I'll find Evelyn, who will show me where to load, complaining in a gruff voice, as she does so, about how "the boys" never know where anything is and how she is going to show them someday and not come in, and then where will they be and with her back the way it is she can't lift anymore—and where are those men anyhow?

At Lake County Nursery my first stop is at the office, where Linda greets me. I may stop in to ask Ned to hold the five witch hazel cultivars we had discussed on the phone or find out when my second order will be dug. At the dock I feel very insignificant among the rows of cavernous semi-trucks being loaded to go out of state to New York, Pennsylvania, Illinois, and elsewhere and with the Bobcats wheeling like beetles as they stack trees onto landscaper's trucks and trailers. But up in the dock office, which is elevated and run like a flight tower, with a view over acres of nursery rows, I am greeted by name. Sue glances at the long list of plants on the order sheet and asks if I think I can fit everything in.

"With my big car?" I ask. The joke is that I used to come with my Honda stationwagon, and the amount of material we loaded was always a source of wonder. Now I have the Toyota van, so very little is left for a second run.

"I forgot. You never leave anything anymore."

Then Les calls across the huge office, "Valerie, when are you going to get yourself a pickup?" The dock staff has been urging this on me for years.

The help who load have nothing but the most brute labor to perform all day, starting at daylight and going until dark and in all weathers, heat, cold, rain, mud. In fact, one of the fantasy correctional programs Kris, Nancy, and I dreamed up for the arrogant is a month's work at a nursery. These young men and women are possessed of a graciousness lacking in many people who consider themselves superior. The grammar may not always be correct, but they are smiling, friendly, and helpful, traits as out of fashion as the lemon lily. I am always in awe of the goodwill, the muscle, and the care taken by the men who will fit any trees or shrubs into the van, layering the balls one on the other so nothing is damaged. And if by chance a plant is not perfect, a replacement is found.

Jane is a marvel at nursery stacking containers, so when I send someone else for a pickup, I can pretty well guess how much to order knowing about what Jane can fit in the van. We've spent hours together tagging for special clients, selecting the healthiest or best-shaped plants, Jane dragging them out of the rows and herself pointing out imperfections. We might drive to a plot where there are plants she wants me to see. How she can remember my tastes and interests with so many hundreds of plants and people I find more amazing than the innkeeper who knows the client who prefers marmalade to raspberry jam for breakfast.

At Klyn's, Amos comes into the office to greet old friends while I bombard Bill Hendricks with questions I've been saving for him. Bill is my plant guru, and it is to him I go to find things like the elusive sapphireberry or sweetfern. I save him seeds of my Clematis

verticillata and try to talk him into producing the wild thorn apple, which I am in love with but can't buy for those clients who would appreciate a whiff of real spring. These plants produce a delicate yet heady fragrance that shames any of the nursery hybrids. As I am a client of one for such wildlings, I haven't been able to talk him into commercial production—yet.

The thorn apples, gray dogwood, and black locusts are among some of the wonderful wild plants that are ruthlessly trashed by the bulldozer. It may be because we still have so much that is wild in this country that we do not value what nature gives us; nor have we yet come to realize that what comes in on its own is right for that place. Our highway department, for instance, has decided on a beautification plan, for which I give them credit; but they could command greater beauty at no expense if they stopped mowing. Immediately, the plants that tolerate salt or gravel or wind or clay would claim their territory in a tapestry that the cleverest designer would find hard to equal.

If either Bill or I have the time we go out to one of the poly houses, Bill talking nonstop while I try to take notes. It is by looking at some of his favorites, or juveniles, listening to his descriptions of habits and soil requirements that I have been able to introduce plants to my clients that I would never have heard of otherwise. Best of all, he keeps up with all the new ornamental grass introductions, and it is to his nursery I go to assess those I've read about in horticulture magazines.

As I believe in massing the grasses, using different heights and foliage to play off each other, I usually need an empty van for that pickup. We stack them in until the swaying fronds turn the van into a mini prairie. (Once, when I stepped out from my "prairie" to pump gas, I overheard another driver saying to a buddy, "Will you look at that, she's growing grass right in her car.") Real self-indulgence comes for me midsummer, when the pressure of planting is off but the perennials are in full bloom and the trees and shrubs are showing their best foliage and form. Now I can afford the luxury of field visits, instead of the rushed in-and-out pickups of the planting season, when I leave home at dawn to be at the nurseries when they open so that there will be time that day to plant.

With appointments made, picnic and water packed for both of us (Amos always comes with me), sun hat and notebook in tow, and lists and catalog in hand, I set out for the day. I have two lists. One is of plants I want to see growing, perennials to inspect for habit or color and shrubs for leaf, bark, or flower. Another is a list of plants I have read about or seen used by designers such as John Brookes in England or Mien Ruys in Holland or native plants that have been recommended by American ecologists or plant propagators.

My first stop might be Springbrook Gardens, one of the largest perennial growers in the country, where I can see new introductions, often natives or hybrids of natives, or new German cultivars. With the first list I have only to be pointed in the right direction. With pencil and notebook, Amos and I walk the rows, with our good intentions to keep to business lost as one color or shape after another calls for inspection. The hot sun, the summer breeze and acres of flowers dissolve any remaining discipline, and I give in to the sensual pleasure of wandering alone through the silent spectrum of an orderly company. The hum of an unseen tiller in the distance only makes my intimacy with these fields of plants, fields of color, fields of life more profound.

When Amos's panting reminds me how hot it is, we retreat for an hour to the riverside park before visiting another nursery. There, while Amos swims, I loll on a log in the shade and find that I did take notes after all. Gaura lindheimeri—"very graceful, ask about winter hardiness." Artemisia 'Valerie Finnis'—"use this, all it is supposed to be." Euphorbia myrsinites—"try this for S., should do well in that dry situation." Potentilla fragiformis—"lovely foliage here, semi-shade?" Platycodon 'Florist White'—"good new white flower, is it as vigorous as 'Mariesii'?" Next visit I'll have Dave Schultz, owner and manager of Springbrook, settle all the new questions, but my head is too full of impressions to tackle the practical now.

Amos keeps up his puddling, carrying out rocks and sticks from the bottom, while I admire the cut stone foundation of the old bridge and think of the care and art the settlers put into their building.

The afternoon heat settles in, and I know it is now or never if we are to continue the day. Off to another nursery.

The next appointment will likely be in the office with my second list. Depending on the nursery, the office may be air conditioned, but Amos is always invited in and given a welcome and treats by the secretaries. The discussion takes place as we check off my questions one by one. Some of my question plants are being propagated but are not of commercial size yet; others will never be propagated by this large nursery, but another might be into it. Inevitably we get in the nursery truck to look at something that has to be seen in the field. It may be lined out on a plot two miles away. It doesn't matter. We'll bounce over the dusty nursery paths to look at it and other specialties on the way. By the time I head for home, I feel as I do after spending too long in an art museum: my head is spinning; I'm physically exhausted but at the same time elated and excited. I hit rush-hour traffic going south on the freeway, but the slow pace is right for my frame of mind, as I am already planning where to plant that Pyrus salicifolia pendula—but what about fire blight? Must ask.

About the Pinus sylvestris 'Fastigiata' there is no question; it is just what we need for C. in that small area outside the dining room window.

One of my favorite stops in Lake County is at the nursery of Horace Wilson. The fields are tucked behind an old Western Reserve farmhouse sheltered by the original maples. Seldom is there any sign of life, as even his help, a young fellow of seventy-eight, is usually back in the rows. But at all times of year Horace will be in the fields where he has been growing unusual plants for seventy years, and you will only find him by searching the nursery. It takes a while, but it is not lost time, as there are always eye-catchers to comment on or ask Horace about when I find him. Often he will be in a row setting out new seedlings. Hard of hearing and with failing eyesight, he takes a few minutes before straightening out his lean, frail frame to smile a welcome. Once I have told him what I'm looking for, he tucks the unplanted seedlings into the soil and we amble off to find it.

This is not a quick-stop place. On the occasion I've brought a time-conscious client to look at a tree before buying it, I could see in him what the Mainer must have seen in me when I asked directions—nervous haste. Answers are deflected by forays into rows of plants the client has no interest in. Horace, who barely sees, seems to know by instinct where the holes from dug trees are and says casually as we short-cut across rows, "There's one that has to be filled," while I try to save the city-slicker client who never thought that looking at trees for his yard might mean avoiding muddy pits or ruining designer shoes. At the same time, I'm trying to jot down Horace's descriptions and comments. The fact is that if you can't find what you want at Horace's, you probably won't find it anywhere.

Just one example is the fringe tree. If I want one of any size, I go to Horace. This is one of our most beautiful native trees and one that is difficult to find, at least here in Ohio. The feathery, fragrant blooms in early June have earned it the common name of Old Man's Beard, and as it was a favorite of Thomas Jefferson it is an appropriate plant for historical settings.

At Horace's nursery the client can look at eight-foot Amur chokecherry trees with glossy cinnamon-colored bark and zone-2 hardiness; a gray-barked weeping beech; a Carolina silverbell, an underused native tree with ridged and furrowed bark; big Pagoda dogwood; and some of the hard-to-find maples, like hedge maple, which is tolerant of compacted soil, and Manchurian maple and Nikko maple; and the evergreens—fastigiate, weeping, spreading, yellow, blue, all shades of green. I need a day just for this one nursery, and with it my notebook and my bible, Michael Dirr's *Manual of Woody Plants*.

In Horace's own yard, planted years ago, we can study mature specimens. It is easy to see that there is more to a tree or shrub than foliage. We can look at the red exfoliating bark of a fifteen-foot paperbark maple, and a client, looking at a fifty-year-old specimen of the Scotch pine, can understand what I mean when I speak of the angularity and bark color, or how lacebark pine gets its name. I can show a huge spreading bottlebrush buckeye and magnificent specimens of Chinese dogwood and of course rhododendrons and all types of holly.

But Lake County is only the beginning. There are many other plant people and nurseries to whom I owe so much information and visual memory. There is the iris breeder in an Akron suburb, a little old lady whom I came upon while she was resting in the middle of an acre of flowers of exotic beauty. The colors of these butterfly-like blooms mingled like the colors of an impressionist painting, and there in the midst of this scene was the seated figure in straw hat and galoshes—just as if she were posing for a painting. There are all those specialists—Hal with his variegated plants; the bonsai grower with an Ohio backyard turned into a Japanese garden; the old rose specialist who explained to me the process of propagating roses; the fruit tree, soft fruit, prairie grass, and wildflower experts; Jim Bissell at the Cleveland Museum of Natural History, who leads botanical wildflower tours in downtown Cleveland—and so many others whose life interests have enriched mine.

One of my most indispensable connections is near Medina, with Rhonda Jones, who runs Lafayette Greenhouse. Because of Rhonda I have been able to provide my clients with unusual annuals. It all started with the blowzy petunias I saw in the containers at my oldest daughter's farm. They turned out to be California giants.

"Where did you find them?" I asked when I first saw them. I had never seen anything so 1920s, so buxom.

"That's what I want to tell you," my daughter said. "There is a greenhouse down the road and it's run by the nicest woman who really seems to like plants and who's interested in trying new annuals. I think you should meet her. She might even be able to grow things for you."

That was all I needed. Within minutes we'd left the dogs behind the fence, put the last horse in the paddock, and taken off for Rhonda's greenhouse.

That was the beginning of a friendship with a very special person who has expanded my horizons through her intelligence, thoughtfulness, and generosity of spirit.

Usually before Thanksgiving we will meet at Rhonda's with our catalogs. It is an easy drive on the freeway, with views of unpretentious Ohio farmland, ponds, large stands of woodland accented in this season with gray beech trees or the leathery maroon leaves of oaks. In the ravines the sycamores spread rugged white-mottled branches as markers to water courses. Before the Medina exit there is a panoramic sky view that reminds me of Ireland, where the skies are ever changing and where light streams in shafts through the clouds.

Rhonda is no housekeeper, so we sit at one end of her sofa that is cluttered with books and, for these consultations, more catalogs than I knew were printed. First we analyze the plants of the past season. Some, despite praise, were not successful. They may have burned out in the heat or were not the color described, or they might be better used in hanging baskets. Others I want never to be without. Of the latter category I try to estimate for Rhonda how many flats I will need—how many six-packs, how many four-inch pots. This is real guess work, as I never know until the season is well on who will want what.

It is not until we have gone over all this that we settle into the new finds. Rhonda has picked some she thinks I will like, and I've numbered pages of flowers I want her advice on, a distillation from Thompson and Morgan, Select Seeds, Canyon Creek, Prairie Nursery, Wildseed, Rockknoll, Wayside, White Flower Farm, Busse, Meleager, Bluestone, Burgess, Henry Field's, Burpee, Park, Harris, and more. There are really very few new plants either of us wants to gamble on in any one year, as now we have a full repertoire of excellent performers. But at planting time Rhonda will always have a new little secret which she gives me to try, as she knows how hesitant I am to plant for others what neither of us is sure of.

Through the years I have been able to offer to my clients some lovely annuals at the time unavailable elsewhere. Everyone's favorite is the small but strong Blue Pearl petunia. I had one very opinionated client who told me she loathed petunias and I was not to introduce any into her garden. She made it sound as if the petunia might corrupt her more aristocratic plants. Then one summer day she walked up my drive to stand over me, while I was on my face pulling weeds, and say accusingly, "Why didn't you give me some of those dear blue flowers you have growing on your bank? You know how I like that color."

I straightened to admit the awful truth—that those dear flowers are petunias.

"Well, I want some anyway. They don't look like any petunia I have ever seen," and she marched back down the drive.

Rhonda has grown mignonette, Dahlberg daisies, jewel-like low snapdragons that defy our heat, the single purslane so loved by bees, the tall Blue Horizon ageratum that offers a tangle of blue all season, stately celosia cristata (her seed came from Monticello), heliotrope (which I plant near terraces for fragrance, "like Mother's angel food cake," one friend described it), lemon-scented signata marigolds, classic zinnias that never stop blooming, and more. And this was before any of them were being grown for the mass market.

Rhonda admits to having no self-control when it comes to ordering seeds, and although she and her husband have added a new greenhouse almost every year I've known them, they are always overcrowded. Her parents, who live next door, help with the pricking out, watering, and sales. Even so, her life seems to go from one crisis to another. There are the late frosts, the unexpected high winds, the early or late season that influences buyers, the flu at transplanting time, or the disaster in the greenhouse.

She called me one March day, breathless. "I have really bad news for you and I hope it won't upset your plans too much. That's why I'm calling now, to give you a chance to look somewhere else. There was a mouse in the greenhouse and he ate all the marigolds."

On another occasion she called to tell me in the same breathless voice that—*pause*, while I prepare to hear the worst—the petunias in the four-inch pots are so beautiful, the best they have ever been at this time of year. Only Rhonda would bother to call two days after I have left with a vanload of annuals to warn of frost, or in the middle of summer to know if I had been affected by the tornado she heard had come my way.

Rhonda gave me advice about planting one of my favorite plants, purple loosestrife (Lythrum). In some states it is banned because it can become so invasive that it crowds out indigenous plants such as cattails, which provide food for wildlife. Rhonda, who is a scientist and even conducts her own tissue culture propagation, has the answer. The hybrids, even though they may set seed, are noninvasive because they have been bred from the North American native strain, Lythrum virgatum. It is the European introduction of Lythrum salicaria that has become so invasive. It is, according to Rhonda, like banning tea roses because the multiflora is invasive. Lythrum is such a stunning plant so adapted to our climate and so versatile that I cannot imagine being without it. Now I feel at ease planting the hybrids, 'Purple Spires' being one of my favorites. I have had no problems with these plants getting out of hand even when planted near ponds—and I have been watching them. My advice is not to dig up the roadside flowers, as that will certainly hasten the spread of a pernicious invader.

When I go to Rhonda's for a pickup, it is always late in the season (annual planting time in Ohio is Memorial Day), and I am already utterly exhausted from the spring work. But this chore is like visiting family. Rhonda's mother and father bring the flats to the car and help me pack my salvaged banana and apple boxes and stack them. We catch up on news—for us, health, weather, business—and commisserate over our exhaustion, as they are even more burned out than I am. Even harried as we are, Rhonda and I go off to look at a few special plants tucked in the back. By the time I'm ready to set off, I feel as if I am leaving after a lovely Sunday picnic, with the van loaded, Amos curled up on the front seat, and the whole family waving goodbye and good luck as I pull out the drive.

Farther south, almost to Wooster, is my next source of inspiration, assistance, and quality plants—Quailcrest Farm. The drive is beautiful at any time of year, but in early summer it is a delight to take Route 83 exit past Medina and into what seems like the heartland of Ohio. Driving south, I go through the town of Burbank, where I mentally restore several old buildings on the main street and wonder why a light was installed, as it seems to be the town that time forgot. (We have a lot of them in Ohio.) By now, too, I have my favorite farms. What is more nostalgically romantic than the ample late-Victorian farmhouses with porches, long windows, green lawns shaded by sugar maples, and backyards filled with an assortment of outbuildings, the whole complex dominated by a magnificent barn, often with louvered windows and roof cupola. The space—the size of lawn, the size of house, the size of the barn, the extent of property—are peculiarly American. I must remind my-self that these are farms built and run by farmers, not wealthy land-owners. In another country they would be princely dwellings. These houses and barns were built with thought and care by craftsmen us-ing local stone, wood, or brick and were meant to be handed down from one generation to another, as many have been until now. They are testimony to the availability and productivity of the land in an age when growing food was an important family occupation, not merely a corporate business venture.

The field crops in this area rotate among corn, soybeans, and al-falfa; so depending on the time of year, I can see vast tilled fields, ei-ther deep brown from new turning or new green with sprouted grains. If I go down in June or later, as I often do, now that con-tainer plants make all-season planting possible, the roadside flowers are in bloom—the chicory that lines the roads like a painted band of blue, Queen Anne's lace, and orange ditch lilies, which I can buy now at Quailcrest. Our attitude toward these "invaders" is chang-ing; we are beginning to invite them into our homes and give them legitimacy with names and birthplaces.

The thorn apple bloom is long over by the time I go to Quailcrest, but the black locust, which colonizes many roadsides, may be in bloom with its fragrance strong enough to reach me even on the freeway. In June, though, the heavy scent is from the multiflora rose, now in disrepute because of its invasiveness. I roll down the windows and drive slowly to prolong the "high" of this aromatic trip.

Quailcrest is also a family operation, but it is a big family. Libby and Tom Bruch bought a dairy farm when their four children were small and took on country living as a better way of life. The dairy has long since given way to a thriving herb and perennial nursery run and maintained by their now-adult children.

Each has his or her own domain according to interests. Debbie runs a sophisticated garden gift shop. To meet the six-foot-four-inch Toby, who is in charge of herbs, you might think that he tended oak trees instead of the intricate knot garden that is his own creation. Ginna supervises the growing of perennials, and Rusty is in charge of any remaking of gardens or walls or fences as well as the shrub and tree department. Libby and Tom fill in everywhere and supervise; after all they had the original inspiration. I tell my clients to do what I never seem to have time to do, and that is to take a day to visit Quailcrest; meander in the beautifully maintained gardens, browse in the gift shop, examine the knot garden, wander through the greenhouses, and certainly don't miss the show room for plant and garden ornament treasures. The final treat is to picnic in the shelter or on the lawn under old trees.

Is it my fantasy about a place and people I am so fond of, or is it true—that on those lawns there is always a breeze, the summer days are never too hot, the gardens are always at peak, and no one is overworked?

# CHAPTER 4

# The Barn

THE BUSINESS WAS WELL under way before we were reintroduced to George. It was Helen who brought him home one evening after a concert he was recording and she was photographing. He looked familiar, she said, and after all she had heard about him from her sisters. It took us hours that night trying to catch up on the last twenty years. Helen was the only one of my three daughters who had not passed through George's fifth-grade class.

"Tell me, did you really allow kids to bring snakes to school? Did you teach them the oboe? What was it you brought in wounded that had to be fed all day, a chipmunk?" Helen wanted answers to the stories she had heard from her sisters.

That spring Helen would take George on her night photography rounds of Cleveland. It could be anything—architectural shots, bridges, the Terminal Tower, the Cuyahoga River, warehouses, deserted streets, and bars. She took him to a city few Clevelanders know anything about. And when they returned at 4:00 A.M. she would go to bed and George would join me on the predawn dog walk. As we walked around the ponds or through the fields, I'd hear about the night's adventures, of what good photos should result, of the throbbing beat at the bar, of Helen's ability to take photos that no one else could because she seemed a friend not a voyeur.

It wasn't long after meeting George that he invited me to tag along on some of his jobs. As a free-lance recording engineer he could offer treats to chamber and symphony orchestra concerts, organ recitals, and even German beer hall bands in recital halls and churches throughout our area. I reciprocated by including him on some of my jobs, handing him the mattock and pointing out the stakes where the holes had to be dug or the manure spread.

The most unique recording studio, however, is George's own house—the Barn. As a result of my association with George and the Barn, a landscape job evolved, one that tested all the theories about staying in harmony with the surroundings.

The Barn. It sounds rustic and simple, and it is—in the way you might say the pyramids are simple. It took five years to build. The architect was an eighteenth-century farmer; the artistic reconstructionist and engineer was George. The Barn was built from two endangered eighteenth-century log barns taken from a southern county and reassembled in an eleven-acre woods near Kent, Ohio. The atmosphere is set by the winding, quarter-mile drive that's reminiscent of access lanes to northern lake cottages where branches brush the sides of the car and small animals scurry out of sight. A cabin is what one expects at the end, not the looming structure with timbers that look as though they grew up from the leaf floor of the surrounding woods and were then, laid like giant Lincoln Logs. All the grim stories of pioneer hardships can be seen in those hand-hewn beams, some as long as fifty-two feet, the length of the building. The surrounding trees, magnificent as they are, are but spindly mockeries of the giants felled by that early farmer from the virgin forest he turned to the plough. These logs are reminders of what he found when he claimed his land from the Indians, of hardship but also plenty, for these forest giants did not go into fine furniture or a fancy house but into shelter for his animals.

The entrance into what was originally the threshing floor is approached up broad sandstone steps (salvaged from a Cleveland mansion), onto a large porch, through a handcrafted front door, and into a windowed mud room. From there another door leads into the threshing floor, the central vault where the wagons hauled in the hay to be pitched into the lofts on each side. What a breath-catcher! Still open to the roof, this volume of space is exaggerated by an entire wall of windows that look out onto the woods.

There are no real partitions. On one side, six steps up, the old hay mow now houses the grand piano and is the setting for many recording sessions. Under this and on a lower level to the threshing floor, into what would have been the pigsty, is "the snug," a quite separate space with a wall of glass on the north and long windows on the south. This room and the kitchen are the only "private" rooms in the barn. On the opposite side, the corresponding snug space is now, by stepping down three steps into the original animal stall, the kitchen. A staircase with no railings, leads up from the kitchen and across a bridge—no railings—to the bathroom, dressing room, and study. For the sure-footed there is yet another level leading from here to a platform that hangs above the threshing floor— just a platform, still no railings—which makes for a great place to listen to music, read, or lounge. The final level, the sleeping loft, is reached from here by climbing a ladder. The barn is not a place for those suffering from acrophobia, but it is wonderful for children and cats, who use the cross-beams like a giant jungle gym.

Because they are not defined, the various levels seem to float in space—it can be disorienting to see chairs that seem to be neither hanging nor resting on anything solid. It wouldn't surprise me to have the magic meal of the fairy tales appear in space before me ready to taste. In a way it is also disorienting to be so close to nature yet in a house—not just the outside so closely viewed from within, but the logs, which despite the huge windows, create an atmosphere of living in a hollow tree. Probably only homesteaders live surrounded by such strong natural elements.

There is always something new to discover in the logs, almost like the living tree. Now neatly chinked, they reveal their individuality like portraits of tough ancestors, through knots, bumps, rough or smooth places. No mill gave facelifts to remove the age lines and wrinkles of these timbers of oak, cherry, maple, walnut, chestnut, beech, whatever trees had to be cleared for the plough. Just as character is tested through time, after two hundred years the wood has become iron hard, the marks and skill of the hewer cut in forever.

If looking at the logs evokes the past, even more so they are testimony to an incredible vision on the part of George. Vision and tenacity. How was he able to haul them all here from their hill in Coshocton County? To reassemble them, chink them, fit windows, do the plumbing and heating, and install all the other modern devices unknown to the original? And how was all this done while still keeping the integrity of an old log barn? But there it stands, a monument to the past and the present.

The serenity at the Barn is complete, the air filtered by trees. Here tree frogs announce spring, the dank soil tickles the nose after a

rain, the deer pause to browse on the back ridge, the fox trots purposefully in his search for rodents, the December mating call of the owl terrorizes the forest, and dogs must be confined when that pungent odor warns against the chance encounter with a skunk.

The drive switches back to another structure built very much like a tobacco drying shed, which at 44 x 48 feet has more than enough space to serve as garage, workshop, and storage. Just in front of the cedar-shingled "annex," as it is called, is one of the few cleared and partially sunny areas on the property, a place where George planted what he calls his garden, a collection of salvaged Siberian iris, roses, mallows, phlox, monarda, and others, which take on unique shapes and flower forms in their struggle for light.

Given this setting, what landscaping could be done? None, in the usual sense. What we did do was clean up. Debris had accumulated from the building of the two buildings that had to be raked, shoveled, and carted off. This, I felt, equaled the monumental work of the original construction, not only because the trash consisted of piles of roofing slates, timbers heavy enough to be moved with a winch, cast-iron pipes, odd sinks, various pieces of rusted equipment, but all of it was of value to George. Any one thing mentioned needed only a bit of repair to function like new, so of course it could not be parted with—like a wheelbarrow that was perfect but for the absence of a wheel. Even the leftover scraps of rotted timbers could have solid bits cut from them, I was told. So the cleanup became a job of finding a place to hide a lot of unsightly metal and wood, and the few vanloads George finally agreed to part with were wrenched from him and mourned over later, things like broken roof shingles, scraps of lumber and pipes, unusable plumbing fixtures, and odd, incredibly heavy machine parts.

At last, with a nice empty space in front of the annex of about 50 x 30 feet, we decided to gravel the entire area, not just the drive to the annex door. In this way the neat clearing, a contrast to the shaggy surrounding wilderness, might even be turned into a sort of garden. Which is what happened.

There was still a lot of stone left from the Cleveland mansion, so with some of it we made a retaining wall for George's garden. Encouraged by that we set up a stone bench and then wedged in a pedestal to mount the millstone as a table, with three stone stools surrounding it. We used more stones to mark off our new garden from the car drive, and when it was all finished we celebrated by serving tea from the millstone table and sat back and admired our work.

I couldn't believe what we had done—just the two of us. This project introduced me to the spud bar and tunneling bar. George put his physics to work using balance, levers, and a lot of muscle. When a stone was really big he would say, "We'll walk this one." It sounds so easy! Don't believe it. They had to be raised, grunt by grunt, with wedges to hold each new few inches. Finally they were worked on end—balanced, George reassured me. "Don't fight it—let it hang there." Fine and good if you weren't afraid of being crushed to death, which I was. I have no affection for the spud bar, which represents something beyond my control, unlike the mattock, which is a real helper. Let's face it: every stone we worked with was too heavy for anyone except August, the stone mason extraordinaire. But it was done, and now the other side cried for attention.

"It would make a terrific sculpture garden," I said as we stood looking at the clean gravel expanse and thinking of our friend Jenny's abstract stone animals.

"What about the radiators?" George pointed to a stack of odd-shaped iron poking from the undergrowth. Their weight had saved them from being hauled away with the rest of the debris. I had learned not to discount George when it came to using found materials, so we hauled the radiators out for inspection.

He was right. We were soon assessing each one for shape and size—some were narrow and tall, others squat, one flat like a grill (perfect as a foot wiper at the entrance to the tea garden, as we now called it). The twins with prominent feet, if turned upside down, seemed made to hold the big sidewalk stone for a table. Suddenly the radiators became works of art that we struggled to set in just the right place, moving one over a few inches, another tipped on its side, and one reset to show the fading paint. Somehow we arranged them and even walked, balanced, and wedged the 4-x-3-foot sandstone slab in place. And so the radiator garden was created. It is the perfect place to read on a summer day or to lunch from the stone table or just to hang out.

George's flower garden struggles not only from lack of sun but from smothering invasive plants—they are not called weeds, and George won't pull them. The result is a subdued wildflower garden with only a touch of color: a single red rose is more spectacular in that tangle than an entire bush of roses, and white phlox and a few deep-violet iris splatter through the green. It all complements the radiator garden, both nongarden gardens.

Spring is when I like it best there. Then the little iris reticulata come up through the gravel to hug the millstone pedestal; the forget-me-nots and violets, out from the woods, spread through the rusted iron of the radiator garden like a bit of fallen spring sky. But best of all is the coltsfoot, which displays itself around the big southern Ohio chimneypot and along the edges of the drive, even before dandelions, which the yellow flowers resemble. The fluffy seed heads follow when the plant is still without foliage, and around the dark chimney tile they are like a fur muff, which is transformed into a summer necklace of large round leaves. What more can one ask of a plant? The reason coltsfoot is so little appreciated can only be because it grows anywhere of its own will, which of course makes it a weed—unwanted. I was vindicated when I saw it used as an extensive ground cover in a Mien Ruys garden in Holland.

George has another volunteer, poke weed, one of our native "weeds," which for strength and architectural structure could not be bettered by any plant. At George's it grows in powerful company, right against the annex next to a huge steel sculpture by a local artist, Ira Matteson. Pokeweed is another much-treasured American plant used as an ornamental in European gardens. For the rest, gardening at the Barn consists of periodic clearing of brambles and undergrowth, which, if unchecked, can make for a stifling atmosphere in summer.

On the south side of the Barn itself, the kitchen door opens level to the ground. There is one paving stone at the door then the rare pleasure of bare ground to walk on or to place the bench, for this is an early spring sun trap with a view onto woods, ferns, and daffodils. It was sitting there that I realized how seldom we walk on bare earth or even grass. It is the designer's delight to go to as many convolutions as possible to keep feet off the ground. A deck or patio is a status symbol, depending on how elaborate it is, how many levels can be incorporated, or if a hot tub can be included. Yet, what is more pleasurable than sitting or stretching on grass, or placing chairs and table on grass for dining or tea? Here at the Barn the bare, swept earth "patio" creates an elemental, primordial pleasure, the sense that we are touching the sustainer of life, Mother Earth, as Kristine would say.

But it would be impossible to offer such simplicity to most clients, which makes spring or fall sun sitting at the back door of the Barn all the more precious.

# CHAPTER 5

# *Pools*

$A$LL WINTER I'D BEEN toying with the idea of putting a pool in my front yard, my inspiration coming from lectures I'd heard in England by designer Anthony Paul. Even given the differences in climate, I was sure that some sort of water garden would work here in Ohio. But when I consulted with local contractors and garden specialists, the comments were all negative—"they're a lot of work to make"; "they always crack"; "mosquitoes, algae, green slime . . ."; not worth it—until I spoke to the experts at Tricker's, a long-established Cleveland water garden firm. They sold the rubber liners I had heard about in England and more or less assured me success. At least there would be no cracks.

As soon as I made the decision to turn my front yard into water, doubts set in. It had been easy enough to tear out my front lawn for the cottage garden, but now to tear out this garden I had worked so hard to create—could I really do it? All for a pool I was not sure would work. Could anything, I wondered, replace the delight of the herbs and the flowery profusion we enjoyed from the new front porch, from the earliest species bulbs to the late Clara Curtis chrysanthemums, falling unstaked over the wall? After all, if a plant doesn't work it can be moved with very little effort; it would not be the same with a huge hole in the ground. To change this, if it proved a mistake, would involve more than I cared to think about. I really didn't know if it would be even an equal trade-off, but it was something I felt had to be done. There was no way that I could recommend a water garden to a client if I didn't try one for myself first.

As with the original decisions for my College Street garden, I had to decide on the style. It would not be one of those formal pools of European gardens, not the stagnant so-called lily pool, not the farm pond, wonderful as it is. To replace my cottage garden I would have to have a cottage garden pool, with lilies and bog plants, fish, and oxygenating plants—the water equivalent of what I was giving up.

My nephew Roger was up from Florida for a visit and wanted some work, so I romanticized to him and Helen about what fun it would be not only to have a pool but to make it ourselves. I made light of the work involved by saying that I had dug so many holes for large trees that it didn't seem such a big deal to dig a bigger one in the front yard. It would be a fun project. Helen could work on it when she had time out from the darkroom, and I could help as my schedule allowed.

"You're serious," Helen said when she came home one day to see most of the front garden circled by the clothes line, an irregular 10 x 14 feet. "You think we can dig all that out? It'll take a lifetime."

"We'll all work on it," I insisted, "and the weather is cool now—good working weather." It was the end of February, and the day alternated between freezing rain and snow flurries. "It won't be too bad." We stood shivering in our coats staring at the marked-off space of sodden leaves and brown humps, the only promise of flowers. "Only one end has to be as deep as three feet," I said easily. "Then it can slope gently up where we can cut a shelf for the bog plants."

"Wait till I tell Roger. Three feet! Do you know how deep three feet is?"

"Just about three feet," I couldn't help answering.

I was wrong. When you are pitching clay up from the bottom of a pit, three feet is more like six feet.

"Anyway I've thought it all out. We leave nine feet between the porch and the pool. This will allow room for a bench, a few pots, the edging plants and a stone surround." The final vision focused in my mind. "The bench can go over there. There will be space to walk all around, and tall bog plants will be beautiful there." I pointed to a clump of brown sedum heads.

It was the synthetic liner that had so encouraged me because it meant that we could build the pond ourselves. Just dig the big hole; lay down this heavy nontoxic, ultraviolet-light-impervious liner; fill with water; add fish and water plants. It seemed like a beginner's recipe. No concrete experts, no men with diggers that wouldn't fit

in our front yard anyway, just our own familiar tools—shovel, pick-ax, and wheelbarrow. After a lot of my romantic waxings on the beauty of ponds, Helen and Roger admitted that it would be great to have a pool in the front yard, but they never did fall for the idea that it would be easy. They had been caught in too many of my projects. None of us, however, realized just what we were getting in for.

"Before we start digging I think we should have all the rocks for the edging on hand," I suggested.

"Not more rocks!" Helen had helped me haul rocks for the retaining wall.

We returned to those abandoned farms and stores of salvaged sidewalk stone and scrounged from a contractor who was "improving" a terrace in town. "I don't know why you don't take up china painting," Helen said as we struggled to get a huge slab we thought we couldn't live without into the car.

Then the digging. We borrowed the truck from my oldest daughter, who lives on a farm near Medina. George offered to take the clay for a fill on his property, and the precious topsoil enriched the beds in the backyard. With time out for bad weather, it took Helen and Roger two weeks to dig out the hole and carry off the soil.

To speak the verbs makes light of the labor. Dig. Shovel after shovel. Easy at first in the loose soil, easy enough to encourage then deceive. Soil turns to clay, then to compacted clay, jokes become curses, and dig becomes pick. How dainty that sounds! Roger in the pit, visible only from the waist up, rose several inches with the force of every strike of the pick from an overhead swing. Helen finally gave up the shovel and threw out huge clay clods with her hands.

Carry off. That sounds easy too. The truck was parked next to the wall. When the wheelbarrow was filled (the challenge was an overload), it was run down a plank that stretched from the wall to the edge of the truck, across the plants on the bank, then tipped up and emptied. The trick was to empty it into the truck, not all over the street. The balancing act with a wheelbarrow of clay was as precise as riding a unicycle on a tightrope.

The weather—cool weather is good working weather, but what about rain and sleet? Clay and rain equal glue—and a no-work situation. During these spells until the clay dried out enough to pick again, we returned to what passes for normal for us, with lots of dinner table jokes about my bog and what a good advertisement it was for the garden designer to have a slopping clay yard.

But the hole was finally dug—three feet at the deep end, enough depth for the fish to overwinter, with a slope at the opposite end and the bog plant shelf, all according to plan. Now, after the grim work, the fun could start. The liner could go in. The very day we were ready to lay it down, I found a quantity of carpet pad set out for the trash. Just what was needed to be laid around the sides and on top of the four inches of sharp sand Roger had tamped in the bottom. The stones for the edge were ready in the yard and there was all the gravel from the original garden for leveling.

Helen and Roger did the "laying in." We were going to find out at last if it was going to work, if it would hold water, if the liner measurements were correct. I called it excitement; Helen and Roger only thought of the consequences if it didn't work.

"Hey Roger, it'll be a lot easier bringing the clay back to fill in the hole than it was digging it out. It's all loose."

"Hell yes. We'll be able to load in a couple of hours and have time left to hit the bar."

"No, Roger. We'll be able to fool around with those barn stones that were too big for the Honda. We can start a wall in the back, that way it would be farther to haul them."

And on and on.

Finally the liner was unfolded over the protective carpet pad, and brought up over the edges. Then we half-filled the pool, which allowed the weight of water to settle the liner. So far so good. Roger spent the next two days fitting the rocks in. The first course was put on the liner, which was brought up behind, like a partial wrapper, and the excess trimmed off. Then the second course was set to cover the first stones and liner and overhang the water by two inches. This meant an enormous amount of fussing. The level is crucial, and it was difficult even for someone as precise as Roger, because no two stones were the same thickness.

The day the pool was filled, we called George over from the Barn and Helen made a pasta with mushroom sauce for a dinner celebration. We hunched down at the new pond's edge in our slickers, unaware of the raw rain. Magically a picture took form like a photographic image in the chemical bath: the reflections of the maples across the street came up and were laid across the water distorted by the drizzle and breeze. There was our own Monet painting. After all the bad jokes, even Helen and Roger admitted that it was an unqualified success.

"You saw it all along, didn't you old Mum," Helen said affectionately.

Helen added the fish, Roger the bubbler and I the lilies. From this first day the pool became the focal point of our lives. It is ever changing and ever exciting. Why had no one told me when I was asking about pools that I could be mesmerized by fish, that I would plan my day to watch lilies open, that a front yard could become a nature preserve?

My first act in the morning is to look at the pool just below my bedroom window, a slice of heaven and earth, a reminder of all that we are part of. There lies that patch of water, bright or dull according to the day, holding its life forms to itself. From above I can see the orange flash of fish and the lily buds; the night bloomer may still be open, its fragrance mingling with the land scents of Rhonda's heliotrope, old-fashioned nicotiana, and mignonette. In this way the new day speaks and gives me a chance to come to terms with it. Whatever happens out in the world, there is this pocket of serenity to return to—the fish will still be cruising and the lilies blooming and stretching their long stems.

The year we installed the pool we had our first severe drought. But there is no drought in a water garden! Here, all I had to do was top up the pool from time to time and water a few pots, then I could sit on the porch and relax with a clear conscience—no weeding. Once planted, the miracle of growth took over without my help. The water lilies, in deep pots of garden compost topped with gravel, grew and bloomed with a vigor only to be compared with Jack's beanstalk. In the bog, the slender stems of dwarf cattails and yellow flag contrasted with the round leaf marsh marigolds. The fish spawned and a frog came from God-knows-where to sit on a lily pad like an illustration from a book.

That first year I had been afraid that the pool surround would look artificial and bare, so I put in some annuals, some of Rhonda's small-flowered portulaca with soapwort here and there as a perennial cover. I had no idea that portulaca is such a delight to bees. Both portulaca and the day-blooming water lilies close at night, so in the morning the bees wait like ladies for the doors to open at a sale, some tearing at the lily petals to hurry them on. Once the flowers open the bees take over, and the planting, rich with color, now has the added delight of sound, that gentle hum of bees in flowers that is the essence of summer. I wish I could taste portulaca honey—would it be aromatic or strong? So many people are afraid of bees, but they are the most single-minded insects, and unless molested or stepped on, the last thing they will do is attack humans. I found myself scheduling appointments for late morning in order not to miss this early drama.

The front yard pool was marvelous, and the fish wintered over as we had been told they would. They go dormant in cold water and hang near the bottom hardly moving and not eating. But the tropical lilies are like garden annuals, and in our climate they must be replaced every year. Now I have more hardy lilies that do not have to be removed and show green shoots in the very early spring. The tropicals, however, are so beautiful and fast growing that I cannot resist adding one or two every year just as I would garden annuals.

The following year, riding on the success of the front pool, I tentatively broached the subject of putting two pools in the back. I had expected the idea to be thrown out, but even understanding the work involved, my slave labor took me seriously enough to offer suggestions. That at least was hopeful.

"The only way to do it is to bring in a Bobcat," Roger assured us. His previous year's visit had evolved into a full-time business as a carpenter, building custom garden accessories, everything from fences, arbors, and benches to a carriage house. Clients considered themselves lucky to be able to book him, and I considered myself lucky to be able to recommend him. "No way could we dig all that out," he added studying the now-familiar clothesline circles.

"So where are you going to get a Bobcat?" Helen asked.

"Rent one. They have everything at that rent-all place. Those things are great. I watched a guy use one when I was working on that big fence job."

It was the same freezing weather. And in addition to the clothesline for the pond outline, there were four stakes to mark the position of the garden house, which was to be set back into the lilacs at a slight angle. It would have a deck across the front and it was to look as if it had been there forever. Roger had volunteered to build it in his spare time—that was before I decided that the garden house would be incomplete without a pool, that the deck had to hang over water.

Every job we undertake involves more than we count on and, digging the back ponds was no exception, mainly because there was a slope that was hardly noticeable when it was in flower beds. The idea was to link the ponds by a waterfall, a small riffle down a rocky gully, but this meant creating a dam and leveling each pond separately.

Roger was grinning like a schoolboy when he brought in the Bobcat and took the controls. I, too, had seen these machines and thought that it would be the greatest fun to have one (the only machine I have ever felt friendly toward). They are like a child's toy that actually works, and nothing seems difficult for them. They turn on themselves, go anywhere, and even come with augers (to dig those big tree holes), blades, buckets, and other amazing helpers. They are the landscaper's Cuisinart.

"Just watch this baby work." I was as captivated as Roger and secretly thrilled to see this friendly creature in our garden. It was wonderful to see him jockey it back and forth in such a small space and move the soil with such ease. We wondered why we had slogged so over the front pool, digging it all by hand. As he pushed the soft topsoil to one side the rest of us—Helen, George, and I—wheeled it away to use on beds or dumped it in piles to be used later for containers. At this point Roger was in charge, excited by his new toy, raising and lowering the bucket like a pro, making tight turns, easing it back and forth.

"Hey, maybe we should get one of these," he shouted above the motor. "We could take on a lot more jobs."

The words were no sooner out of his mouth when he hit clay. It was damp, and sticky as glue. The tracks spun as if they were on grease and then stuck. Roger dug with stubborn fury, ticked that his machine was letting him down. So much for the Bobcat.

Helen was laughing, always ready to make fun of a man, especially a man with a machine. "Good thing we didn't make a down payment on one, eh Rog?" she called.

I was a nervous wreck, thinking that the blasted thing (it had suddenly lost its benign aura) was not ours and had to be returned at the end of the day. But if we ever did get it out, I knew I'd use that clay base and puddle the pond the way they do in England. After all, if clay can be used to seal toxic waste, I certainly could use it to seal a pond. George was trying to help by giving a physics lesson on balance and leverage. Our artist friends from down the street turned up to see the progress, laughed with Helen, went over the layout, and left thankful that it was not their problem. We were wrangling over what should be done, Roger feeling to blame and getting very tight at the far-too-many suggestions, when who should walk in, jaunty as a prince, but August, followed by his man Greg.

August is an artist with stone—if you can get him to work. It's not that he's lazy; he works harder than any human I've ever known. But he lives on the edge. His machines always break down. He has desperate accidents—the kind movers of tons of rock inevitably have. His men leave, as they must. And so forth—one misfortune after another. But there was August today, out of the blue, to deliver a rock he had promised months ago. Naturally I rushed to him as the one person who could get the Bobcat out of its hole. After all, August's life is spent making machines do his bidding.

"Let me in there, Rog," he said with authority. He swung into the cab and then grinned up at Greg. "Remember gettin' Big Red outta that field?" Greg nodded with a grin and pulled his ball cap lower. "This is no more than spittin'." August put his hands on the levers. "Now, Greg, you, Rog, and George sit in the bucket and we'll get this bugger outta here."

The three men climbed in to hang on while August ground back and forth. Helen and I stood on the sidelines laughing. Finally the Bobcat rose out of its pit to a general cheer. And when August climbed out like a liberating soldier from a tank, Helen dashed in for the beer. Settled easily on humps of clay, the group made the decision that the rest would have to be "finished by hand." It sounded as easy as hemming a skirt. I looked around at the devastation to the once-lovely garden, at what had been done and what still had to be done, and it was all I could do not to burst into tears. It was like those photos of London in the Blitz—a huge crater surrounded by the remnants of civilization. To make the scene even more pathetic, there were early bulbs flowering through heaps of soil, bulbs which, I now told myself, should have been the forerunners of a joyous spring garden—and now look at it. It was too much. I had to leave the scene.

There was a lot of talk about how to proceed. Depressed as I was, I realized that we were too far along to give up.

"Don't worry about it," Helen encouraged. "The front was worse.

What makes it look bad is that everything that's been dug out is still there. We have to have a system and do one job at a time, and I say the first thing is to get rid of all the clay." When Helen takes charge there is no one like her. "That means getting the truck back— George can we borrow your wheelbarrow? We need two. Good. Roger how much time do you think you can give to it? You can? Great! Well," turning to me, "I don't think that it will take all that long. What about deep-dish pizza for dinner tonight? Roger, you want to go to the grocery with me and run the dogs?"

And it was done—just like that. Not that it was easy, but the result has been a small pleasure garden of great magnitude.

With his genius at carpentry, Roger really came into his own with the garden house. He had the 8-x-10-foot structure framed in no time. The narrow end faced the house and the deck did hang over the pond, or it looked as if it did. (In fact, the overhang is no more than eight inches.) It was sided with silver-gray boards from an old shed, and the frames of mullioned windows salvaged from an old house, two on each long side and one at the short ends, were painted peacock blue. George found a weathered door from his salvage stock, and Roger satisfied my desire to hear the rain by roofing the house with tin. Over the rear half he made a loft and a window in the peak—for moon viewing—and below it a built-in seat long enough to stretch out on. The seat was eventually covered with masses of pillows, and an old table and chair completed the furnishings.

I was in love with the idea of garden house before it was ever built, but when it started to go up I couldn't believe how wonderful it was, and now that it is finished, I can't imagine living without it. I rush home to nap there on summer afternoons, to watch the fish or read or watch the cardinal feeding its demanding offspring in the lilacs that press in around. I breathe in the perfumed air and let it enter the pores of my skin like an expensive cosmetic. In the heat there is the drowsy afternoon throb of insects: the thrum of cicadas, the insistent crickets, and the gentle hum of bees that invades slowly, first into the subconscious and then becoming as basic as a heartbeat, to be taken up by one's own inner rhythms.

In a rainstorm every nuance of the weather shivers through the tin roof, heightened by the scratching of the lilac branches against the metal or rubbing against the old boards. There are the first ten-

tative drops, the fury of the heavy rain, and then the slow easing off, almost drop by drop. The snug shelter takes on the character of a nature blind, where I can look out through the door to watch the lily pads gyrating like moored boats and watch the water jumping in the pelting rain. Here I can have my own sea voyage firmly tethered to solid ground.

Pathetic, I often think, that so many of my clients are jailed by their air conditioning—no scent, no caress of a breeze over the skin, no sounds of birds or insects, not even the close up progress of a rose over the door or buds developing and unfolding. How they work to afford all the things that stifle the senses, and finally, with enough success, to be cast off completely like an obsolete tool.

The top pond, near the garden house, is held at one end by the dam covered with large stones, the pathway to the deck. The water runs from the top pond to the lower under one of these rocks and down a pebbled runnel. A pump in the lower pond circulates the water to the top where it spills back over a rock. The sound of water from both the spillway and the rock splash is very gentle. Tall grasses and cord grass at one end of the top pond add to the sense of enclosure. At the base of the grasses are marsh marigolds and creeping Jenny. Actually, the marigolds and creeping Jenny have taken over the edges of both ponds so that there is a yellow glow almost any time of year. The iris I've planted in a container so that the foliage can rise straight out of the water. A little Japanese maple that I couldn't resist at the nursery will eventually hang over the end of the lower pond; and because height was not desirable there, the maple is surrounded by Lady's Mantle. Of course, there are water lilies and fish and now toad and frog choruses every summer night that inevitably result in masses of tadpoles. Where do the frogs come from, and what happens to all the tadpoles? Surely the fish cannot eat them all. The toads I find in the garden all summer, some no bigger than a little fingernail.

Every year the ponds are different depending on the weather and my experimental plantings, but always they are a fascination.

Now, anyone for a garden pool?

# CHAPTER 6

# *A Picnic*

WHEN JENNY CALLED for help with the outside of her new house, I knew it wouldn't be like coping with Mr. Fret, whose phone calls were so constant I regretted installing the answering machine. It was like being tailed. With Jenny, the challenge was to make an intimate space with very little money. No elaborate hardscape, no mature plants brought in. Anyway it's fun to help a friend, especially one who is sensitive to nature and has an artist's eye. Appreciation of Ohio Nature 101 could be skipped.

Not possible with Mr. Fret, who when he asks what a tree looks like in winter, I know is asking if it will be green, not whether it has bark or structural interest. Most homeowners are the same, insisting that evergreens be planted first, usually blue spruce, although there are very few places in our area where they fit in easily. I am not totally opposed to planting evergreens, but they are best used with restraint. Mostly our surroundings are deciduous hardwoods, of which Ohio boasts more species than any other state, and if left alone they provide unmatched beauty. The hardwood-forest ecosystem varies with the seasons and provides as well as new saplings understory trees, ground covers, and wildflowers that would take years to replicate. But I have to point all this out to most of my clients.

Perhaps there is little appreciation for the native hardwoods because it means getting out into the woods to know them. From a lawn or deck, a woods just looks green in summer and stark and dead in winter or "all brown and messy." The current practice is to cut out all undergrowth, all understory and saplings, to leave an inhospitable environment for any ground covers or woodland flowers. As nature abhors a vacuum, weeds or brambles move in unless the landscaper piles on the mulch—which he does at regular intervals.

The more affluent the homeowner, the more there will be of these sterile mulch islands set into the chemical lawns. Often someone realizes that this effect is fake, so rocks are added as an offering to nature, which only compounds the aesthetic horror. Certainly it doesn't relieve the unnatural look of brown mulch under remnant oaks or maples or bring back the smothered woodland flowers—trillium, wild geranium, dog-tooth violet, hepaticas, May apples. If a homeowner finally decides there is too much monochrome brown, then hostas are planted. What a pathetic substitute for the intricate, self-sustaining planting proven through eons of trial and error that has been ruthlessly wiped out!

We are accustomed to putting nature at our beck and call—if we can have strawberries in January, then why should we put up with a brown Ohio winter? But there *is* interest after leaves turn and fall, it only takes a change of attitude and a willingness to empty our minds of the clutter of malls, lights, and sounds that overwhelm our senses in today's world. If we let nature's low rhythms flood our consciousness, then our perceptions are heightened and the ordinary becomes the extraordinary.

So, for a client like Mr. Fret, who insists that he wants everything "natural" but who nevertheless views the winter landscape as a blight, and is unaware of anything except leaves or no leaves, green or "dead," I explain about bark, shape, and outline, and to make my point we go together to Horace Wilson's nursery.

On the drive out I take a roundabout route to point out specimen trees I have noticed on my drives, to show him their architectural qualities, perhaps in a venerable white oak, an old apple tree, a stand of sumac, or a giant catalpa. The roadsides and fields we pass are cut over land or abandoned farm fields of second-growth shrubs and trees and have their own beauty according to the season. If it is early enough in the autumn, the gray dogwood retains its gold-dust-yellow leaves; later, it stands straight with pink-tinged tips. The grasses and wildflowers pattern the fields in swirls of umber, burnt sienna, and coral accented with the gray bark of red maples against bright redosier dogwood. Where they have colonized banks, rugged black locusts and sumac, with its scarlet furry fruit, add to the natural beauty I point out.

"I like it, I like it." In his excitement, Mr. Fret becomes more twitchy than usual, and I begin to think that I have made a conversion. "What should we get? What do you think would look right out the living room window toward that mess in the back?"

The "mess" is an uncleared second-growth tangle of shrubs and trees that originally he wanted to cut down and replace, as usual, with pine trees. I encouraged him to build on the existing vegetation. He was receptive but unconvinced, thus the circuitous trip to the nursery. Together we selected serviceberry, several good-sized Carolina silverbell, deciduous holly for a wet spot, and the common winter beauty redosier dogwood. In another damp area with more shade we planted a group of seven summersweet to add fragrance. These plantings were layered like material in a collage against the existing canvas of wild crab, hawthorn, viburnum, red maple, and, in the sun, multiflora rose. The location for this type of planting was perfect; no houses in sight, just a clearing in first-growth vegetation.

By augmenting what was there with a small collection of native shrubs, even though there were no specimen trees to preserve, the view is now enticing. There is anticipation instead of green sterility. Birds, butterflies, and mammals have not been evicted and the area is vibrant with life.

I have had other converts who tell me that they see differently now and even have questions about wildflowers (which they used to call weeds) that they've seen from the freeway.

But many more cannot be converted to beauty that is not provided by color and tidy, controlled shapes. Perhaps it is only in the garden where we have control; where, living in neat rows of a correct size, we can see what we "own," have paid for. Here we can pronounce the death sentence without trial—heads can fall, limbs are severed—or we can indulge in magnanimity through banishment. There is also the subliminal fear that nature in the end must be conquered or it will get the better of us; nature is, after all, to do our bidding.

But this wasn't Jenny. Her house is in a lake community that has changed through the years from summer cottages to winterized summer cottages. They range from downright trashy to prim, with as much variation in owners. There are college professors, artists, artisans, workers, and out-of-workers. It was the perfect place for Jenny, a writer and stone sculptor, to find an affordable house with space for her stones. The smaller stones she had brought from La's yard in Hudson, where we had seen her working on them. (La is her artist mother and our good friend.) They were now stashed in the garage until a new place could be found for them in what we both hoped would be a sculpture garden.

Roger had been working all winter on remodeling the house. The interior had been gutted and with Roger's meticulous craftsmanship a breathtaking space had been created; a loft over the kitchen, and a miraculous play of light and shadow that falls on the soaring white walls from the original cottage windows. The wonderful thing about the house is that it remains on the outside a simple cottage, which heightens the drama of stepping into a very contemporary room, and this, along with Jenny's needs, dictated very simple landscaping.

Jenny and I had looked over her garden one very cold February day when everything is at its worst after the winter snowmelt. The backyard, which is on the north, has a square of about 20 x 20 feet formed by the rear wall of the house and the garage projecting at right angles to it, which creates a dank pocket. Beyond the garage wall the yard tapers to the rear in a pie shape. Huge oak trees shade the house to the south and east. As we looked at that uninviting square, I mentally eliminated the half-burned trash, sodden leaves, and bare cinders and saw only a private gallery for Jenny's sculpture.

"What you need," I said, "is a feeling of enclosure. Why not gravel this whole area? Grass would never grow here anyway, and it would be such a great setting for your stones." I walked the perimeter of the two sides opposite the house wall and garage.

"Sounds great," Jenny said, "but really hard to do. I mean gravel—how would we do it?"

"No problem," I assured her. "We'll rally the troops. It'll be a picnic." That phrase dismissed the labor of spreading gravel. "Now along here we could have a fence or hedge of some kind with an opening, maybe a gate or arbor, into the rest of the yard. That way you could have two separate spaces, like two rooms. And with the gravel near the house it would be so clean and uncluttered, beautiful for sitting out in the summer and a real showplace for your work."

As we wandered the rest of the property, trying to define the lot line, I put it together in my mind. The front yard, dominated by the oaks, was to be fenced for Casey, Jenny's pretty border collie. The

problem was that awkward shape to the rear. It wasn't really an eyesore, but it didn't relate to anything and was uninviting.

"We have to enclose this rear lot so you'll have something to look into from the gravel yard," I explained to Jenny. "What we could do is build a bank of tough shrubs that will fill in quickly, shrubs like lilacs, honeysuckle, viburnums, and maybe some old roses that would arch over with fragrance and color."

Jenny was smiling. "Great, just great, and look," she turned toward the house, " I'd see it all from the kitchen."

"Later you could sink stepping stones level with the grass for a visual lead through the arbor to a bench set among those old roses."

"That would be so beautiful" Jenny was grinning now, not even aware of the raw wind. We were both thinking of summer luxuriance, a bench and fragrance and a breeze stirring the leaves of the big oaks. It was rare to talk to someone who could catch the same sense of place even on an impossible day, in an impossible situation, and transcend it all to inner visions of beauty.

"But wait, Jenny. It won't happen all at once." I had to give fair warning. "If we are being frugal we won't buy the largest shrubs, and even fast-growing ones take time to fill in."

"Oh, I don't care. I know it will be beautiful and I would rather watch them grow."

"I'll have to quote you to some others I work with who want everything at mature size immediately." It was true. "How long will it take to grow?" was a frequent question. No one wanted to wait five minutes for anything, as if gardening were no more than selecting the living room sofa.

"I know the perfect hedge for you and it won't cost a thing." My mind was on the enclosure for the gravel garden. "We'll just dig your hedge from the wild." It sounded easy. "It's a wonderful plant, gray dogwood, and the bulldozers are trashing them where all the new developments are going in around Hudson." I explained to Jenny how much I liked this plant; its stiff upright habit and cut-off height meant that it needed minimum pruning. In winter it has a very gray cast, and with new spring growth it colors its habitat with a rosy top glow. It is one of the many plants I admire as I travel the countryside wondering why these native treasures aren't treasured.

"It'll look as if it belongs here, and there will be no maintenance.

Now what about an arbor? Would that be too much do you think, if it is very simple?" Jenny is not the cute type, and I thought she might think an arbor just that.

"I love arbors. That would be terrific." She is an artist, after all, with the ability to visualize. "What would we grow on it?"

"There are so many things. I have a rose that is surefire, Viking Queen, and she lives up to her name for taking our winters and coming through the summer non-stop with deep-pink, very fragrant blooms. Best of all she asks for no sprays, just lots of manure in spring. With her, a deep-purple Jackman's clematis looks spectacular."

Only now did I remember the arbors I had had specially made for me that were standing behind my garden house dismantled. One of them would be perfect for this low-key setting. A welder had made them to my specifications. The metal arches, rusted to a rich brown, were designed to attach to posts the width of the opening. When I described them, Jenny approved, and I promised to find the posts to attach the arch to. I ended up with locust posts of just the right length for the arbor and dropped them at Jenny's on my way to the barn. (Locust is the very best wood for fencing, far outliving treated lumber according to my old-time fence maker in Kirtland, Ohio. It is no wonder that our forefathers, from George Washington at Mount Vernon to our early Ohio farmers, planted locust groves.) Everything seemed set for the installation—everything except those gray dogwood Helen and I were going to drag from down the road where new building was going on.

"It won't take any time at all." I thought that I could cheer Helen on. She was so leery of any of my projects, especially if I said they were easy—with reason, I had to admit.

"You don't expect to do anything in this weather?" We had been having the usual foul February with cold, sleet, or snow flurries almost every day.

"We certainly can't wait around for summer. Anyway this couldn't be better for transplanting. Cold and wet."

The plan was for Helen and me to dig the dogwoods—just pull them out—drop them off at Jenny's, and then on Saturday, Jenny's day off, plant them and do the whole of the gravel garden in one day.

We coordinated the workday with La and George as this was to be a communal effort—all of us rallying to help get Jenny started. I ordered ten tons of sand and twelve tons of pea gravel to be delivered on Saturday morning. The sand goes down first to hold the gravel and give it something to settle into. The work gang—Helen, La, George, and I—were to be on task by nine with shovels, rakes, and wheelbarrows.

The Thursday before that Saturday, I insisted that the dogwoods be dug; twenty was what I figured for a nice hedge effect. Naturally, in order to keep my masochist reputation with Helen, that Thursday was a bone-biting raw cold, complete with snow squalls.

"Well, we won't be digging today," Helen said, pouring a leisurely second cup of coffee. "Good day for the darkroom though."

"We can't possibly wait." I answered. "And it's really not bad; in fact, it's the very best weather for transplanting, no stress for the plants." "Transplant," I thought, had a more friendly ring than "dig."

"I knew I should have left for the Greek islands," Helen lamented. "With one life to lead and here I am dragging it out in mud."

What she said as the day wore on I don't want to repeat; but to give her her due, she kept up a fierce pace. The trouble was that the shrubs didn't just pull out as I had thought they should. No, they had to be dug, or chopped, the roots cut, and all this in a sucking mud that held the spade, the shoes, and the wheelbarrow. The latter we finally abandoned; we ended up dragging the plants up a rough hill to the van. Even stacking them was hard, as they were all so sodden; and there seemed so many of them, many more than the twenty we finally counted. We were soaked to the skin, and our boots so caked with mud we had to take them off before getting into the van.

"Let's go right now and drop them off," Helen said. "But Christ! Turn up the heat! Maybe we can dry out on the way."

"Couldn't agree more. To have to face this mess tomorrow would be more than I could take."

Twenty minutes later we were at Jenny's where we had to wheelbarrow the plants to the backyard. All we could think about by now was getting home to a hot bath and a pot of tea.

The Saturday workday miraculously slipped in between the snow flurries and cold rain. We couldn't have had a better early spring day: brisk with wild scudding clouds that made the uncertain sun welcome, warm enough to be comfortable and cold enough to want to keep working to stay warm. Made-to-order weather for moving ten tons of sand and twelve tons of pea gravel. Roger, who was still working on the interior, was considered too skilled to waste on grunt work like moving gravel, so the rest of us set to, each moving from one job to another as we tired. First, the trash had to be raked and put in the dumpster. Then the sand was spread over the rear square, wheelbarrow by wheelbarrow. By the time that was done, we were all starving.

La had promised us lunch. We dropped our tools when we saw the bright weaving spread in the sun on the new sand, just as if we were at a beach picnic. Ever the artist, La's lunch was a visual as well as gastronomic treat. No cheap plastic containers of store-bought potato salad or iceberg lettuce. Baskets held gourmet treats of artichoke and crabmeat salad, potato salad with an indescribably good mayonnaise, marinated green beans, crusty loaves, and other delicacies. I ate so voraciously I can't even remember what they were except that each was more delightful than the last. The floral plates were a paper equivalent of English Spode, with a predominant cornflower blue picked up by the paper napkins. When the champagne cork popped, Roger popped at the same time—right out of the house, dropping his carpenter's apron on the way. From that moment he stayed on as a member of the grunt crew, and without him we would still be moving gravel. The champagne glasses were glass, and always full. The ambiance was more like that of a grape harvest in Alsace than a Saturday afternoon in Brady Lake, Ohio.

The afternoon work went at a very cheery pace until at last the gravel was moved and none of us could believe that it was only four.

We had been so involved with getting the job done we hadn't noticed the total transformation. The gravel square was enclosed and intimate, inviting and clean. The arbor had been installed, and the new hedge looked as if it had always been there.

The following week Nancy, Kristine, and I planted the shrubs for the rear; two American cranberrybush viburnum, lilac, mock orange, flowering quince, and three fragrant old-fashioned roses (two rugosa Sir Thomas Lipton and one Therese Bugnet). For the gravel yard we introduced a dogwood in the shaded corner under the oaks and on the opposite side, where there was more sun, a bent Japanese maple.

We planted the Viking Queen rose for the arbor along with purple Jackman's clematis.

Jenny's was as instant as a garden can be. Now the rear shrubs are filling in. The dogwood provides a resting place for birds coming to the feeder, and several stone sculptures have found homes along the garage wall. It was an unusual project because it was all volunteer, and perhaps because of that and the unpretentiousness of the house and setting, the garden has become a model of simplicity for others who believe that it takes a lot of space and money to create a garden.

# CHAPTER 7

# *August*

THE HEAVING SIGHS of those air brakes were unmistakable. I looked at my watch. Just past four—not bad. The appointment had been set up for eleven but, with the lashing rain and August's reputation I didn't really expect him at all today.

I pulled on a slicker and went down the drive to meet him. He was just crawling out of his enormous crane truck and his helper was parking the big red dump loaded with rocks for the Cleveland job.

"Had a real bad time loading. That's what held me up," August said. On the ground he was dwarfed by his machine, but he looked as much master of it as a lion tamer his lions. If he had been wearing sequined tights instead of jeans and a sleeveless tee, it wouldn't have surprised me to see him make the truck breathe fire. He stood, feet apart, square—square shoulders, square face, big square hands—there was no mistaking his strength, although he is not very tall. August has the physique body builders would envy. But it's been built not in dilettante gym workouts. He's developed his muscle over years spent wrestling rock and timbers. His work is salvaging old buildings—barns, churches, stores, houses—before they are buried by the bulldozer. In the two years I had known August, I had seen him with a beard, mustache alone, or clean shaven. Today the mustache was back. Usually he wore a sweatband around his forehead, and his jeans or coveralls were a miracle of threads holding together in just the essential places. There was about his square face, unflinching gaze, and assured manner the look of a gypsy prince. He could have tamed unbroken horses, or he could have played the role of Christ at Oberammergau, because with all his strength there was a vulnerability about him. With all his air of mastery he was never quite master—at least of life.

He lived on the edge. Things went wrong. Trucks broke down—lost their brakes or blew tires or axles. He was always overloaded and trying to do the impossible, to will the old truck to go or to bid on a building or to salvage it. He was always against the clock or the weather or injuries or the odds. He couldn't be kept down. No matter what the catastrophe, he would be back fighting life's bad luck. No one knew better than I the implausible, unrelenting, inescapable misadventures that formed the fabric of August's life.

I had recommended him to do the stone work I had designed into the small but elegant grounds of a new house in a very affluent district of Cleveland. If I had ever suspected that the job would take a year—a year of three-way phone calls (the client with me, me with August), recriminations, threats, name calling, and total frustration on all sides—I would never have let him near the job. Day after day, month after month, it dragged on unfinished, and the most frustrating thing was that all, at least almost all, August's excuses were legitimate.

What can you say when a man's legs have been almost severed by a truck? What can you say when the truck's brakes give out and it is lost over the edge of a cliff? What can you say when a bid has to be made for all the houses on a strip mine property, which, if successful, could provide income for a year? What can you say when it rains or snows nonstop for six weeks, making work impossible? What can you say when the truck breaks down on the freeway and has to be towed? What can you say when the stones aren't delivered because, after a two-hundred-mile trip one way, the quarry was closed?

And what do I say to a client who is hoping to have a completed terrace by July Fourth? A terrace that had been started the previous July. What do I say when the client threatens to sue? What do I say when the client, almost in tears, says August did not turn up yesterday because it was his birthday? How do I answer as she screams over the phone at 7:00 A.M., "My party is in three days and the terrace is unusable and," with voice rising to hysterics, "my husband has had a birthday every year for forty-five years and he has NEVER stayed away from work."

How could I reconcile attitudes toward life that were so at odds? The client: efficient, ambitious, aggressive. August: living from day to day, not understanding why it would be wrong to knock off one job for a few weeks to take on another that might go to someone else. He would finish the work. These people just didn't understand. He had never walked out on a job. But "When, when?" the client shrieked. "Will we live long enough?" And the most frustrating thing of all was that we all knew, August most of all, that there was no one who could do such incredibly fine work or find stones that will never be hewn again. Not only does he have the stone for any job, but he loves them. He talks about the shapes, the scoring and facing, the color, where they came from. He is a poet with stone. Beautiful double-faced stones, cornerstones, stones quarried by handsaw only a few years after the Indians had been banished to the west bank of the Cuyahoga River, flat old sidewalk stones, pink or blue terrace stone, stone mellowed or shaped by a river. But the artistry was in the way he set them. Each was studied individually to show a facing or the best color or a rounded edge.

Yet even with nonstop frustrations inherent in working with August, there were episodes that, despite my irritation with him, made me laugh.

The rainy day when this same client, Mr. Bleek, after a confrontation, agreed to advance a check. These advances were necessary for any of the many reasons that kept August living on the edge. "No way I can haul the load until the crane gets fixed. No way I can bid on them stones I told you about for the steps if I got no money. Had to help out my cousin with a pickup he needed bad—took all I had."

"Come on then," Bleek had snapped. "Meet me at my office, just follow," and he pulled away in his Mercedes 450, August following in the dump truck.

It was rush hour at the busiest intersection—rain, wet pavements. Bleek, ever the harried businessman on the car phone, decided not to try to make it through on yellow and stopped. August put his foot on the brake and didn't stop—couldn't stop. The huge dump was set on course to wipe out the Mercedes and anyone in it. But with great skill, August swung the wheel of the truck as if it were a sports car and saw Bleek drop the phone as the shadow of the dump passed within inches of his window and continued through the intersection dodging the rest of the traffic.

When August shifted down into a space next to the Mercedes in the office parking lot, Mr. Bleek was slumped over the wheel waiting for strength to stand up. He left the phone where it had fallen and staggered out grateful enough to be alive not to be angry.

"When I saw you coming in the rearview, I thought it was the end."

"You know I wouldn't do that to you," August said calmly. "I didn't have my check yet."

For my part, I feel that I have lived more intimately with August than I have with my own children. It was all out in the open. Every day—every single day—wondering about this one job and what new calamity could have befallen August when he didn't show up yet again. It was worse even than getting Helen through high school (and I had thought that nothing could top that for misery).

Now on that gloomy July afternoon, in front of my College Street house, August urged me, "We better get on up to that job. You lead the way. Pokey," he patted his dump truck, "sure don't sound too good today. A short somewhere, so we have to keep her going." He nodded at the throbbing truck as if it were a recalcitrant dog, then swung lightly into the cab.

I called Amos into the van and led the way to La's house two blocks down the street. She greeted me from the studio as Pokey came into her drive scraping the low-hanging branches.

"I never expected him in this rain," La said surprised. She had heard endless August stories. Then she looked toward the sculptures he had come to move. "Do you think they can get in there today?"

Jenny's enormous sandstone sculptures were set up in the yard where she had created them. The one we were looking at, set up on blocks at the edge of the lawn near the shrub border, was the largest, about eight feet long and three feet wide. It was also the wettest part of the lawn. Then there was the croucher, a mere six feet; the griffin, which for August was no more than a big stone armful; the creature coiled in his stone tomb, a small two-by-two; and the unfinished granite an intermediate four-by-four. Before Jenny had her own house, she had set up her work space on La's lawn outside the studio. Various sizes of sandstone were set onto cement blocks by the winch truck that delivered them. Then, over the months, the rest of us watched as the stone blocks slowly evolved into Jenny's benign creatures. There were twins of cats and lambs, the giants we were moving today, and small abstract creatures resting or coiled or standing. Only someone who loved animals and had watched their poses could have turned hard stone squares into caressable creatures. I had sold a few of the smaller ones and felt that anyone who owned a Jenny sculpture was lucky indeed, as it was almost like adopting a pet, but a pet that needed no care. Even selling them I unconsciously selected what I thought and what I thought Jenny would consider, a good home. But now Jenny had her own house and had already taken the smaller stones there to work on, and so La was left with a yard full of enormous creatures awkwardly exposed on concrete block. That's where August came in.

"How do you think these stones can be moved to a place where they will look right?" La had asked me one day. "After all, Jenny can't take them, and they don't look like anything sitting in the yard like that."

"August," was my instant answer. "However, getting him over here is another thing."

La had lived through my stories of the Cleveland job, so when a few days later I called and asked where she wanted the stones set, because August would be coming through the next day, she was surprised and delighted, never thinking that the action could take place so soon.

La and I had wandered her grounds to find the perfect site for each creature. We walked first to the end of the long drive and found several niches in the shrubbery where we thought an animal could crouch contentedly. Then we stopped to assess the front entrance and stone wall.

"It would be a shame to introduce anything more here," I said, studying appreciatively the whole entrance effect to the spacious Italianate Victorian house. It was definitely the house of an artist. Aside from the color (taupe with deep, almost lilac trim and a touch of mellow rose inside the porch), a weathered garden hose of the same rosy color hung on the house like an abstract line drawing. The stone wall with cerastium spilling over the edge held back coral bells, rue, santolia, lamb's ears. Blue lyme grass circled the tall post

topped with La's own everlastings—a bouquet of plastic flowers found in the cemetery dump and arranged like trim for a Victorian hat into the styrofoam crown of a fourteen-foot post. Resting her back against a big locust tree, a nude female torso gazed with the utmost serenity through the coral bells toward approaching visitors. No, I couldn't see doing anything to disrupt the perfect balance and atmosphere of this entrance.

"What about over there?" I asked La, pointing to the far edge of the large graveled forecourt. There in front of a twisted pine was the perfect place for the largest sculpture. "Come over and look." I was excited now, as I could already see the creature in place, reclining, a smug but benign sentry as calm as the nude under the tree.

"You're right." La was thrilled. "It's perfect. It just couldn't be better." We studied the pine backdrop for the sculpture. It was rugged and irregular, twisted through loss of a leader in its youth and strong enough to afford comfort to the huge animal. Neither of us could imagine the big sculpture living anywhere else.

After that it didn't take long for us to decide to settle the six-footer into a niche along the drive half-hidden by shrubs, like a giant cat lying in wait for its owner to return. The only place for the griffin, we agreed, was under another tree, where the drive split to go to the studio. The coiled animal belonged on the stone wall that separated the bone garden from the lawn; there it could sun itself, rock on rock. That left only the unfinished gray granite, which La decided could remain almost where it was just rolled into the shrubs a bit to compliment the gray of the spear construction nearby.

And now here was August, just a few days after I had mentioned La's job to him, ready to move the menagerie. The reason he stopped today was that he was on his way to deliver the load in the dump truck for another Cleveland job. This time the landscaper was doing the work; August only provided the stone, and so far he was on time.

As August backed down her drive, La came out to assure him that the lawn in front of the big sculpture he was to move was firm. "This was a drive once," she explained. "The studio was a garage, so just back down and don't worry about the trees, they get pushed back every time any truck comes in here."

"Will do," August said. "Let's just hope that this baby doesn't die on us. If she does, that's it." La and I looked at each other.

"Do you want to keep going?" I asked La.

"Oh, sure. It's too late now, and anyway I don't think it's going to quit."

"Just remember that you may have Pokey here for a very long time," I laughed, but I knew that it was a real possibility.

August's man, Greg, stood on top of the truck to hold back the branches, a courtesy seldom shown by any man with a machine. August eased Pokey into position to winch up the big stone. La and I watched in fascination as they set the outriggers, readied the winch, and as Greg lashed rather frayed slings around the big stone. It all looked so impossible, even with the winch.

"It's like the building of the pyramids," I whispered to La—whispered, because in the lashing rain, and with doubtful equipment, the job seemed so life threatening, and instinctively we felt we should not distract the performers.

They worked like competition athletes. Each knowing what move to make, with no effort wasted. August worked the levers as neatly as if they were organ stops and, very slowly, the stone rose in the air, Greg guiding it, while La and I held our breath and watched it sway and come in toward the truck very slowly and very carefully. At last it was over the rear of the truck and Greg scrambled up to push it in place. Here it balked like a horse refusing to be loaded. The stone wanted to crouch half in, half out. August pulled and Greg pushed. I felt like putting a lunge line around its haunches. The frayed slings held. If they had not, both men would have been crushed. At last it touched bottom; all of it was safely on the truck.

"I'd say two ton sixty." August flashed us a smile, looking like a kid who had caught a wide ball.

"How do you know?" La asked.

"Just the pressure, the resistance. We moved a two-ton stone last night. You should've seen it. An old one in front of the church down there where I'm working. They're tearing down a church you wouldn't believe. All cut stone." The water was sheeting off August's face as he talked. Greg stood lank as a hound dog next to the truck, waiting for the next move.

August put his hand on the levers and raised the outriggers. "Now, where is this going?" We pointed to the front corner. "Better let me look at it first." He swung to the ground and we followed him to the site. "Okay, here's where you want it?" He stamped the ground. "First, it's not even. No way we can put it down here the way the ground is now. We need it level." He looked around. "Greg get that bucket in the truck." In a few minutes they had made a level bed for the sculpture from limestone scooped from the drive.

Pokey was put in gear. The engine responded but the tires spun into the wet grass. Even rocking and coercing was no good. The ground was too soft. La and I looked at each other in dismay. Anyone else would have been out cursing us for saying that the drive was solid, but August just jumped out of the cab and said, "we'll just pull her out with Big Red."

"Can you believe it?" La asked. "Just like that with no fuss, he's going to pull it out."

Pokey's temperamental engine was kept running while I drove August in the van to pick up Big Red. Within five minutes of our return, he had tied on a rope, hooked up and pulled Pokey to solid ground, and was in place to unload.

The winch was raised and raised and raised into the nearby sycamore. "My God," I said to La. "It won't work. The limbs will all be torn." La and I still made up an awed audience of two for this one-ring performance.

August anticipated my distress at tearing a tree even for a job like this. "She'll never make it," he said looking up at the huge limbs. "Greg, get me the saw in the right locker. We'll just do a little pruning job." He flashed a smile at us, a little triumph of having a card or two up his sleeve.

Next thing we knew August, with a chainsaw in one hand, was climbing out on the winch with the ease of a tight-rope walker. "I always keep a chainsaw with me," he grinned down at us and stepped neatly onto the smooth barked sycamore. I know enough about chainsaws to know that they are extremely dangerous and that hanging onto the trunk of a sycamore in a rainstorm to remove large limbs might be one of the quicker ways to remove one's own.

But it was done. The branches fell and the way was cleared for the winch to lower the stone. August was again at the controls to reverse the loading procedure. Slowly, the huge creature was raised, hanging out over its new space while Greg guided it in place as carefully as if it had been a newborn lamb. Most gently it was set on the ground.

"My God," I breathed to La. "Wouldn't it be wonderful if all living creatures in this world were treated with such gentleness." Gentle was the word that applied to August with his stones. He was a paradox; tough in strength and endurance but with such an inner quality of gentleness that his stones became as living tissue, to be handled with the care of a cat for her kittens.

We all gathered 'round to inspect, watching August circling the stone to make sure that it was level. "It's no good," he said. "If it's going to tip it should be forward, not back." He was right, of course, but at this point we were amazed that he bothered. "What

ALL MY PHLOX

we need, Greg, is more of that limestone and a few bricks." The slings had not yet been removed, so while the manipulating levers were caressed once again, Greg pushed brick and limestone under the monster until August was satisfied. We all circled the work again. This time it was perfectly settled, unruffled by the disturbance of being lifted to a new home, a magnificent creature comfortably lying at the front entrance of La's house without in any way being underfoot.

Now we had the easy ones. They loaded the big croucher smoothly and took it to the opening along the drive. When the slings were put on for offloading, the creature tipped at an awkward angle. Without a word, Greg straddled its neck and rode the animal out from the truck like a new kind of cowboy. It was the first time I saw Greg smile: up on the neck of the powerful cat he grinned hugely and, looking up at him under the peak, I caught a twinkle in the eyes usually covered by the low-slung baseball cap. It was ride-'em-cowboy all the way to the ground. We were all soaked to the skin and cold and it took only this little bit of horseplay to set us all laughing. "Bet you never thought this job would be so much fun," August said.

"Never," we, the audience, agreed.

The rest of the stones August and Greg hand-carried to their new homes. "Not worth using the winch for these little ones," August said as he and Greg carried them across a long stretch of grass to set them.

"Now," La said, "won't you come in for some hot coffee or anything else you want." At La's that means anything from champagne to soda water.

"Coffee sounds great to me," August said, "but first tell me where I can leave Pokey for the night—we'll never make it home the way she is."

"You mean you'll leave that terrific truck in my yard?" La had, from time to time, considered derelict cars as construction material, so Pokey, I could see, had tickled her fancy.

"You'll leave it at your own risk," I warned August. "You may come back and find it a new color or holding a crashed airplane or draped in netting."

"Wish I could leave it just to see what you would do. Too bad, Pokey, maybe when you give out for good on us . . . ." So La and August were left with separate fantasies.

We went in to put the kettle on, and soon the two men appeared in the kitchen in stocking feet, eyes spinning in a daze at the constructions and artwork everywhere in the high-ceilinged house.

"Ain't this something," August caught it all. "This is the real thing. Man, it's all here." La made the coffee, offered Greg a beer, and took them on a tour of what would have been in other times, or with another owner, the drawing room. La uses her house as a giant gallery for her construction artworks, so everywhere there are visual knock-outs, and as many times as I am there I always see something that I've not noticed before. It is like stepping into another world that is at once familiar, because she uses everyday objects in her art, and fantastical, because all those objects are used in surprising ways. It is like a dream where familiar people do unexpected things. It challenges our attention and makes us rethink what we are really seeing and what we have been seeing all our lives every day and for years and years.

In the corner of the living room, surrounded by constructions, is an old upright piano. "Oh no, I may never get out of here." August moved to the piano as if drawn by strings. He opened a box on the bench. "Look at this will you." From the many objects arranged in the box, August hit on four. "A bone, a stone," he laughed, "a rosary, and dice. That says it all. That's life."

For a long time after August and Greg left and the throb of Big Red's motor had faded, neither of us spoke.

"He is just remarkable." La was the first. "And I never asked him how much he charged, but he is worth every penny of whatever he asks. Can you believe all he did? And so darn cheerful. Anyone else would have gotten pissed off and left."

I had worked with August enough to be able to say to La with feeling, "Today you got the very best, and his best is more than you'll get from most."

# CHAPTER 8

# *Turkey Manure*

So what's up for tomorrow?" George asked as he pushed the Rabbit well over the speed limit past a Porsche Carrera. "Do you remember my Porsche," he asked, glancing in the rearview (not at the road but in admiration of the car we had passed). "No, I guess it was the Jag I had when I was teaching." We were driving back from one of his organ recording sessions on the west side of Cleveland.

It was easy to let my mind roll back. The mood of the organ music and mystery of the dimly lit church was still with me. The late hour, the throb of the diesel motor, and line of lights on the freeway made tomorrow seem very far away, but the image of the young, very handsome George driving to his fifth-grade class in a Jaguar wearing a full-length raccoon coat was as vivid as a photo. No wonder the children adored him, my own being no exception.

It had been a long, strenuous day, and at the last moment I had almost backed out of going to this recording session with George, feeling too tired to trail into Cleveland again after all the driving I had done. But as usual it had been worth it. It was a privilege to be able to tag along with George to hear gorgeous music performed by top-notch musicians—my only problem was staying awake after nine.

This evening had been no exception. The music of Bach and Brahms had poured into the empty church with a rejuvenating power. The organist was excellent, and the instrument was one of the best in the country, a Von Deckeroth that had been made in Germany and assembled by the maker for this congregation, Trinity Lutheran Church, built in 1858, now on the National Historic Register. It is one of many beautiful old churches of Cleveland, often slighted today in decaying neighborhoods. The magic of this session with the organist and his music was a privileged private glimpse of heaven.

"What about tomorrow?" George's voice over the diesel pulled me out of a doze.

"It all depends on what you have going."

"Do you need me for anything?" George asked. "You know I like the work if you need me."

It was true. George did seem to like the landscape jobs, at least he was always ready to help; and for someone so skinny, he was strong enough to lift paving stones and able to wrestle any B&B tree into place. But he did have his own work.

"It doesn't have to be done tomorrow, but if you want to work we need to cut back the grasses at Camet. With Kristine and Nancy there, I thought we could do the whole thing in a day—that is, if you can chainsaw them down."

"Sure. What time do you want to start?" George had a lot of experience with chainsaws, clearing for the barn. I was downright scared of them, although I believed Kristine when she told me that she could handle one as well as any man.

"Why don't you come when you're ready, then the rest of us can be doing some of the smaller jobs until you arrive." George was not an early starter, so it was far better for him to work according to his own inner clock, which meant he would turn up about noon.

When I called Kristine and Nancy in the morning to tell them we were on for Camet, they were both relieved. We'd considered another job none of us was looking forward to (pruning for a bitch of a woman who would complain no matter what we did), but Camet is one of our favorite places to work.

"Good vibes," Nancy said of Camet.

"Everyone is pleasant," according to Kris.

"You just feel right out there," George had said.

"Priorities in the right place," was my word.

Camet is a little factory at the edge of Hiram. Its unpretentious setting is in a corner of abandoned farm fields surrounded by Ohio hardwoods. It is at the edge of the college town of Hiram in what is called an industrial park. (There are two other small factories in the park.) Hiram, population about eight hundred (not counting students), is settled on a hilltop surrounded by rolling unspoiled farmland.

Camet president Dick Cornelison, an active environmentalist, had called me in to do a naturalistic landscape job. The original junipers and taxus had not fared too well, and Dick thought that something far better could be done for a factory that made antipollution devices. He was the first client to have any environmental awareness, and I was excited by his commitment. For once I had found someone who was stricter than I about land care. He lived what he preached and was adamant that whatever we did would not involve sprays, either herbicides or pesticides. Great!

On our first meeting we walked the property while Dick explained what he would like to see. He is a tall, western-type man, lean and long striding, and it was all I could do to keep up with him physically or mentally. Ideas poured out. His enthusiasm for the land was contagious and his plans for the future staggering. He was mad about wildflowers but would not use herbicides to eliminate the existing vegetation to prepare the soil for them. He monitored the growth of a number of seedling trees transplanted from the woods like a father marking the growth of a son. Another good sign. He didn't expect to have everything full grown from the moment it was planted. He believed that by caring for the one pocket of this planet he had control over and setting an example in his own life, he might even be able to influence others.

"If just one family gives up pesticides or toxic chemicals I feel I will have done something," he told me as we pushed through brambles to the woods. "We will leave this alone," he said looking through a nice stand of cherry, oak, maple, hickory, and their understory companions of ironwood, dogwood, arrowwood viburnum, serviceberry. "You might want to come through to see if there are seedlings you want to transplant. Then over there we have a little lunch area for the employees. What do you think? What about this bank? I don't want to have to mow but it does look a bit rough now. Let's go on down here. What would you do with this swamp? Then over there we are getting more land. What about that? What are you going to do about the clay around here, I'm told sand will break it up?"

"Sand? Useless," I interrupted. "We need loads of organic matter. Anything. Manure from the horse farms around, or leaf compost. Dairy farms use their own manure. Whatever you can find. The best

way is to put it on in the fall, then by spring with the freezing and thawing it will have perked down."

By the time we had finished the walk, my pencil was a nub and my head a whirl of ideas, his and mine, because Dick is the sort of man who stimulates thinking in others. It was exciting to meet someone who was with nature, who tried to fit in with nature's schemes, instead of fighting to prove human dominance.

The plan I worked out had germinated on that first walk, but it took a lot of time to execute on paper. It is these natural-seeming plantings that take the most time to design. All the usual considerations must be kept in mind—texture, bloom, hardiness, and low maintenance—but there was the additional concern of using real natives or introduced natives. Where do we draw the line? After several phone calls to Dick, I decided that this could not be a native plant museum. We had to compromise. He had engineers and visitors from all over the world and wanted plantings that would look landscaped but easy and unrestrained. We selected a mix of natives and non-natives to offer structure (but not too much) in the midst of shaggy fields and woods.

Before I had even presented a rough design plan, I called Dick to say that all planting would have to be delayed unless we could improve the soil. Had he found a source for manure or leaf compost? I might have known: he could get all the turkey manure we wanted and had already contacted someone to do the hauling when we were ready. It is great to work with a client who is decisive and with whom a "shitty" conversation is elevated to idealism.

Before planting, all the hard clay beds were treated with turkey manure as planned—truckloads of it. The first round we did get on in the fall on top of a rough tilling. In the spring more loads went on and the whole was rototilled again thoroughly. The soil changed from a concretelike surface that bounced the shovel back to soil that, if not friable, was at least soft and full of worms. In such a short time it seemed a miracle.

The final plan for Camet used masses of ornamental grasses and perennials on the banks and across the front, with native shrubs and trees making the transition to existing woods.

A new brick walk was laid across the south-facing facade of the building where the beds were broken by two entrances. In the central bed between the walks to the doors, a gravel path leads to a bench surrounded by fragrant herbs and flowers: thyme, artemisias, feverfew and sage, cleome, and cosmos behind the bench, and coreopsis as filler everywhere. A huge bayberry complements this aromatic planting that immediately softens and humanizes the approach. The west bed was blessed with a lovely river birch at the corner, and to that we added ornamental zebra grass, switch grass, and, where it could fall over the new walk, fountain grass. Separating these grasses is a mass of black-eyed Susans. A gravel path in the east bed runs between giant silver grass at the corner, faced down with more zebra grass on the building side, and, on the opposite side of the path, maiden grass and fountain grass, again where it can hang over the drive with a bed of Japanese blood grass surrounding a huge rock. In summer, following this path to the side of the building is like walking through a jungle; with the tall grasses swaying and rustling in the wind, it's a passage of a few steps through an untamed wilderness.

On the east side of the building is a large level lawn with steep banks sloping to the road. The steepest, at twelve feet wide, runs from the building along the road at a northeast angle. This bank had proved a difficult eyesore in the past, Dick told me, with weeds, erosion, and dry soil. As it was so visible on the approach, it was an important planting area. Bill Hendricks suggested pink fleece flower for just such a situation. He was right. The polygonum has taken over, broken by patches of fountain grass. And with the entire bank planted with daffodils for spring, it is now beautiful all year. At the top of this slope Sedum 'Autumn Joy' thrives under the same conditions with the same grassy companions. At the corner, where the road turns directly north, the bank is wider (about twenty-four feet) with a gentler slope (a hundred feet) to the service entrance. Here we planted a mixture of grasses in a glorious combination of textures. Several of the giant miscanthus with cord grass to cover their knees, groups of maiden grass and switch grass, fountain grass repeated by the road, all interspersed with masses of purple loosestrife. After five years this sterile hybrid has not spread, even to the nearby swamp, which is what Rhonda had predicted when I bought it from her. Despite this reasoning, I don't think that the Lythrum debate will ever be resolved. I met one nature lover who became almost violent on the subject and considered the mention of it an obscenity.

At the top of this bank, edging the lawn where picnic tables are set out, sedums are massed between fountain grass. At the corner, a big stand of Russian sage and blue spirea offer color and forage for the bees. This same combination of plants, with the exclusion of the Russian sage and blue spirea and the addition of a clump of bayberry, is repeated for the next 160 feet along the road from the service entrance to an unmowed field. The service entrance is edged on one side by black-eyed Susans and on the other by daylilies, or ditch lilies.

These same Ohio ditch lilies I wanted massed along the road, but at that time there was no place to buy them—too common. Helen, ever needing a bit of extra cash, volunteered to supply me. Where she went for her collecting, I didn't ask; I only insisted that she not take too many from any one place so that they could come back. For several days she arrived with her car spiked with lilies for us to plant. If they were not so common, our roadside lilies would be as highly prized as they were when brought over by the first settlers. When they are in bloom this planting at Camet is like a tongue of fire edging the road. I often wonder how anyone, even under orders, can mow such an explosion of life when it blooms along our back roads, but it happens all too often.

In late March the grasses and perennials must be cut to the ground to allow for new growth, and that is where we needed George with the chainsaw. So that March day we were working at cutting back the perennials when George arrived, as I had predicted, at about noon. The ease of his swaths through those tough stems was a wonder, but it would never have been accomplished if I had not been there to remind him constantly that this was not the end but the beginning of these marvelous plants. After cutting the tallest he said, "I don't think I can do it. Why don't we just leave them standing?" Even at the end of winter there is something indecent about cutting fourteen-foot bamboolike stalks for apparently no reason.

"It isn't a primeval prairie to be turned to the plough, and I promise that you will be able to do the same thing next year to the same plants," I countered. For George, cutting the grasses was too much like the wanton cutting of trees we see so often in new developments.

It was a typical March day, biting wind but sunny with banks of driving white clouds. We found a place out of the wind to eat our lunch—Nancy her grapefruit, Kristine her brown rice and avocado, and George and I our peanut butter sandwiches. Kristine passed her chlorophyll drink around, which she assured us was good for everything, made as it was from comfrey. As we looked out at the woods hinting at spring and the untamed swamp, we all agreed that it was this sense of the wild that made this a special place.

"Why couldn't more people understand this?" Kris asked. "Anywhere else the swamp would have been filled and the woods tidied."

"Because they want to control, they want power, any way they can get it, even if it doesn't satisfy," George said.

"It's that most people don't know any better," Nancy added quietly. "They are used to lawns and shrubs and that's it."

Later that summer Dick called me in great excitement. "You know I told you that a sewer line was going through—well they're at it now. A mess. But what has happened is that a big area has been dug up where we can plant wildflowers. When could you come out so we can look it over?"

That was how Camet got wildflowers—because of a sewer line. A huge area had been dug along the side of the building, north four hundred feet through unmowed land to the road at the bottom, then along the road in a swath twenty feet wide and two hundred feet long, and even across the road along another branch road frontage.

Dick was beside himself with excitement—the seeds could be put in without using herbicides, the diggers had done it for him. He was in touch with every wildflower seed company in the country, ordering finally from Wildseed in Texas a mixture prepared especially for clay soil in Ohio. Planting was to be in the autumn and the landscaper was to prepare the ground somewhat by disking. But, as usual, he didn't come, and the season got late. So we went out and scattered the seed by hand on top of very rough, hard clay ground and then covered the seed with straw in what I thought, after sowing, was a vain hope of holding it. How any seed could take hold on that hard surface, I couldn't understand, and I reported as much to Dick, who was undismayed. "If we don't get it this time we'll try again in the spring." It took the pressure off me, but I still worried about those seeds, most especially because I knew how much it meant to Dick.

The following March at grass-cutting time, it seemed that I had been right. Nothing was up in the wildflower area. Nothing in April. With lots of rain in May, I didn't get out to look until late in the month. I wandered around looking for shoots and was encouraged by a thin green fuzz. In June Dick called to say that the flowers were spectacular, had I seen them? I couldn't imagine that the fuzz had changed into flowers so rapidly, but that same evening I drove out to be greeted by a field, framed by the swamp and woods, of dancing color. It was a miracle! After all the rain and a cool spring, it seemed that every seed had grown and transformed a clay eyesore into this wild garden. Now we were looking at the annual flowers—the corn poppies in every shade of red, pink, white and larkspur and cornflowers—and under them the new shoots of the perennials that were growing vigorously. Never have I had a garden where the soil had been double dug with compost do as well. This display of annuals lasted about ten weeks, and during that time cars drove past in lines to see the flowers. Of course, I got Helen out to take some photos, and she did just the job I had hoped for: portraits of individual flowers, overall shots, multiple exposures. She tried it all, and ended by selling two enlargements to the company. They hang inside the door, a precious reminder of spring.

The growing of wildflowers is not the simple sprinkling of seeds from a can. If you are not having a sewer line put in, it means that in some way you must eradicate the existing vegetation in order to give your seeds a chance to establish themselves. There have been many experiments with wildflowers, and there is the usual controversy about what is native. Are we justified, here in Ohio, to plant flowers that may well be hardy but not typical, not to be found naturally in this area? By rights we should have gone slowly with suggestions from Neil Diboll of Prairie Nursery, suggestions to plant the true natives. My local authority, Jim Bissel from the Cleveland Museum of Natural History, thinks that, except for once a year, to keep woody plants out, all we have to do is stop mowing. That is certainly true for roadsides, where nature will do a more permanent and satisfying job than the best of human interference. He classes as unworthy the roadside lilies and the bands of blue chicory lining our freeways and, of course, purple loosestrife.

Our planting at Camet was not natural. It was a nonwild wildflower meadow, which means that with the exception of some of the perennials, we would not see these flowers growing naturally in our Ohio fields. They did rouse an awareness, however, that a field of goldenrod could not, and it was stunningly beautiful. In subsequent years the perennials came into their own, among them black-eyed Susan, cousin to the large Rudbeckia 'Goldstrum'; perennial lupine; gay feather; blanket flower; and of course the ox-eye daisy. My own feeling is that the non-natives do no harm. Perhaps establishing natives is better for wildlife in the long run, but if someone really wants the explosion of color from the non-native annuals and is willing to face the reality that they are annuals, then go for it.

It is no wonder that we all love to work at Camet, where there is a dedicated stewardship, a spirit of optimism, and an example to follow. We often say on other jobs, "It wouldn't be like this at Camet"; or, of someone who wants to spray pesticides, "Let's sick Dick on them." And every year, as is true with any garden, we plan to make this "natural" garden even better the following year. Dick takes the lead as usual, through the now-mature beds and the native shrubs that have been added gradually to blend into the woods. We have had drought and floods, but the planting has proven resilient, disease free, and beautiful almost all year. Even when the grasses

and perennials are cut back, the day lilies are soon showing that earliest yellow-green of spring. It's only right that this garden won the
Perennial Plant Association environmental landscape award for the
best garden in its category.

The vision of one man is expressed in the landscaping at Camet,
where stewardship has proved to be more than just a word. If there
are any doubts that beauty in a garden must rely on noxious chemicals, take a drive to Hiram—especially in the autumn, when the
grasses are at their coppery-golden richest, the rudbeckia seed heads
cut dark swaths across the bank, and the sedums have turned to
deep mahogany.

87

TURKEY MANURE

# CHAPTER 9

# *By Committee*

W<small>HAT MAKES ANY COMMUNITY</small> interesting is its people. Hiram has more than its share of characters, even more than might be expected in a predominately academic town. It is a place where the impossible happens through forceful personalities. I know because that is where I raised three daughters; where George taught two of them in fifth grade; where he tutored Roger one summer; where we had fields and streams for wandering, a bend in the river for swimming, and an old mare for the children to ride. It is there, too, that lifelong friends were made for whom there can be no equal.

It was no wonder that I was proud to be called in, almost as an expatriate (I had moved twenty miles away to Hudson), to design a new garden that was to be created where a house had been torn down amid public protest. The destruction had been done in a sneaky way, with total disregard for the wishes of the community. To placate irate citizens now that the deed was done, it was decided to create a public garden on the property in commemoration of the original occupants, the Doctors Hurd, father and son who between them had administered to the community for over a hundred years.

It was a good sized lot, 85 x 190 feet, enough to make an impact, situated as it was on a corner that everyone passed on the way to the post office.

With a strong garden tradition already established in Hiram by the four public gardens created by the knowledge and drive of some of the faculty, this was a natural outcome for the Hurd property. Copper Beech Park is a memorial to a living tree, on a corner lot where another old house had stood. At one time the progressive forces of the village had suggested that the magnificent beech tree, for which the garden is named, be cut to make way for a parking lot. Through the efforts of a faculty wife, who was also on the village council, not only was the tree saved but so was the entire property. Bonney Castle, a local landmark Western Reserve house that had been used in the past as an inn, had been transformed into the English house with companion garden complete with herbs, gazebo, benches, and Shakespearean flowers, all through the leadership of John Shaw, a member of the English department. A late-Victorian double house had been renovated for the History House by Wilson Hoffman, of the history faculty. The brush tangle in the back had been transformed into a meandering woodland and flower garden by Roland Layton, also a historian. On the property of an old Western Reserve house that had been moved to avoid destruction, Jim and Jamie Barrow had created a historical garden, with old varieties dug anywhere Jim saw them growing, from cemeteries to old farmyards. Jim, a charismatic biology professor, had also established a biology station on a farm at the edge of town. In every case, success had come through the conviction of one person with enough dedication to to rally the support of others.

When first asked by Jamie Barrow, who had taken up the challenge of the Hurd property, to attend a meeting to discuss the garden, I was apprehensive. This would be my first job with a committee—not just any committee, but a predominately faculty committee. I had heard enough through the years about academic wrangling, about indecision and back biting—none of which I needed in my life. I said as much to Jamie when she called.

"Y'all just come on over and meet the committee, ah think you know them all anyway—and then see how you feel," Jamie had said. Jim and Jamie had come to Hiram years ago from Alabama via Yale, and although they had made the community their own, their accent set them apart.

The committee was not intimidating, but formidable nonetheless: the wife of the president of the college, Bev Aiuto; the two history faculty, Hoffman and Layton, who had created the history house and garden, naturals on a get-it-done committee; David Anderson, of the English faculty, who, with an innate feeling for spirit of place supported by vast learning, could be aesthetics consultant anywhere in the world; and Bill Laughner from biology, who

loved Victoriana and of course gardens. Jamie was chair. They comprised a formidable group because they were not only experienced gardeners, but they had intimate knowledge of the history of the community and knew what they wanted to create from this one corner. Would I be able to do it for them, I asked. They must be sure before I took the job.

"I don't know who else we would get who knows us all so well and has the knowledge to go ahead with the project," Jamie had said. "I'm sure I speak for everyone."

The agreement was unanimous. So started what was to be the best design project anyone could have. And the committee? Great. It was a new experience to work with learned people who had this off-shoot interest (very nineteenth century) in plants, horticulture, and gardens. With Jamie's practicality and coordinating experience, everyone was kept on task to accomplish the necessary.

Money, first of all. The property was owned by the college, so Jamie made sure that the land was legally donated to what was now to be called the Hurd Memorial Garden. It was decided that the garden should be done in three phases so that funds would be forthcoming as the projects were completed. It was hoped that when alumni and the general public saw what was happening, the garden would generate its own funds. It worked very much as hoped: soil preparation and layout of paths the first year, planting the second, and the enclosures and arbors the last.

The first requirement was that the garden reflect the character and history of the town and college. With the exception of a few early Western Reserve houses, the atmosphere was mainly Victorian, and the garden, it was agreed, should be Victorian in character. This was a challenge in an era of low-maintenance priorities. There could be no bedding out, no changing seasonal plant displays; instead, we would have to create a Victorian atmosphere using hardy plants that would get along with minimal care.

The first submission was a general design. As with all plans, I had to consider who would be using the garden and when, the overall atmosphere and the atmosphere of special areas within the garden, and how this could best be achieved in the design layout. At this stage plants were not considered.

The approved design plan showed the entire property contained by a replica of the "perching" fence that had once surrounded the main campus block, to be entered through an arbor only from the two streets that bordered it. In this way the visitor could meander along winding paths around planting beds, in one way and out the other. As the lot was so long and narrow, I decided to create three gardens of differing characters. The first and largest north section would have a planting of medicinal herbs in honor of the doctors and beds planted so full as to almost screen one path from the next. The center area, in good Victorian tradition, would be a color garden; I suggested yellow, as there are so many good yellow plants and because it is a cheering color in our gloomy winters. The lowest section would be the "wilderness," that wonderful concept so loved by Victorians of plants growing semi-wild. Along the two street sides

the fence, backed by a shrub border, would give a sense of intimacy. On the opposite long side that bordered an asphalt drive, a six-foot lattice fence covered with an assortment of vines was to provide screening.

Once the first overall design plan was approved, we could decide on the details. Fortunately, there were numerous old photos to work from for the design of the perching fence, and as word went out about the garden, various items came to surface from buildings that had been destroyed in a modernization fervor of the sixties. The five globe cast-iron standards that had lit the entrance to "Old Main," the original college building of 1885, had miraculously been saved. A village resident who had rescued the date stones from the same building, donated them to the garden, as well as some of the cut sandstone foundation stones. This was the beginning of the community support that was essential to compensate for minimal funds. The five benches designed into the plan were quickly donated as memorial benches. When it was decided to place an urn in the center of the front circle, Paul Lynn, a student who had won many awards for his pottery, offered to make one at cost to our specifications. (Later I was able to offer several discriminating clients some of his beautifully crafted vessels.)

After all this had been worked out and approved, we tackled the planting plan. For the shrub border along the street, old-fashioned plants were chosen to offer fragrance and privacy when in leaf so that the garden would eventually become an enclosed place for resting or reading, which was in keeping with the other Hiram gardens that, not surprisingly, had evolved as scholarly contemplative gardens rather than flamboyant horticultural displays. Some Victorian favorites such as spirea, mock orange, lilacs, and viburnums were added to hawthorn and ornamental crabs. An old crab from the original Hurd property dominated one corner of one side. It was pruned and rejuvenated and one of the five benches was tucked under the branches that hang heavy with blossoms in the spring.

The central beds, really island beds, as they are separated by paths, were to be planted with perennial tickseed, Siberian iris, mallow, Russian sage, balloon flower, sedum, miniature hollyhock, white mugwort, yarrow, various ornamental grasses, old roses, annual cosmos, cleome, and a Victorian favorite, the castor plant. This was the foundation to be supported by all the little charmers, violets, Johnny-jump-ups, forget-me-nots, thymes, low sedums, annual alyssum, and, of course, bulbs.

The yellow garden was to be cheered by yellow twig dogwood, sunburst locust, golden Hinoki false cypress, and the smaller false cypress. A place was left for sunflowers and fillers of coreopsis, yucca, and other yellow foliage or flowering plants. A break in the yellow was made by the addition of smoke tree and red barberry.

In the "wilderness" I could at last use some of my favorite Ohio "trash plants." In one corner was to be a grove of sumac, which are especially impressive if pruned to expose the angular rugged branches; in the opposite corner a grove of black locusts; and between these groups Scotch pine, which takes on irregular shapes with age. The ground cover under these plantings was to be a combination of lemon lilies and ditch lilies.

An irrigation system has been added, the shrub border now encloses the garden, vines drape the arbors and trellis fence, the perennials attract summer insects, the urn is a real Victorian extravagance of flowers, and people really do wander in and out on their way to the post office, resting on the benches just as they are supposed to do. The garden has a remarkable beauty and serenity and even with inevitable changes, through additions and subtractions, it has proven hardy in our difficult climate.

The committee helped tremendously with all phases, even planting and weeding. Jamie and Jim have put in uncounted hours: Jim bringing in ground covers and directing students, Jamie organizing the whole operation and working herself on weeding. Now the fund is adequate to hire student labor, because even though the plants may be tough, there is always work to do and changes to be made as the garden comes into maturity.

This garden also won a Perennial Plant Association honor award for environmental landscape design. It is no wonder with the dedication not only of the inspired instigators but the support of the entire community and alumni. Bravo Hiram!

# CHAPTER 10

# *The Secret Garden*

M Y SEMI-ANNUAL GARDEN walks with my friend Anne are a pleasure, as I always learn from her, refresh my senses, and reset my focus. Anne is directed by an innate aesthetic sense that allows no compromise, and she gives me the intellectual and visual reaffirmation and stimulation I need to bolster me on my rounds of the pretentious new developments that erupt like sores in fields and woods everywhere. She frequently asks how I am able to cope with people who have no sense of history, feeling for nature, or instinct for beauty.

My answer is that I do my best to instruct, to open new vistas, literally and figuratively, and that I am often met with an awakened appreciation for certain aspects of nature and our place in it. I have learned to take nothing for granted, either practically or aesthetically, as so many people today are isolated from the most basic contacts with nature.

Anne has given years of service to the community of Hudson: working with our librarian to acquire a National Historic District and then documenting the old houses; forming the design criteria for the Architectural Board, the overall Green Plan for the community that saved the center from tract development; drawing up plans for renovations; protesting and usually winning against some of the more outrageous schemes that would have destroyed the integrity of the town. Her drawings of the downtown and many historic buildings are a lasting legacy. But now she had given up. She told me once that she felt that all she had fought for for years had been swept away. I knew how she felt about so many changes, none for the better, but it wasn't true. This town wouldn't be even what it is today if it were not for Anne and a group of like-minded women who moved here in the fifties because of the village atmosphere and were damned if some slick promoter from outside was going to destroy it.

She is a better architect than most practicing the profession, but her greatest artistic expression is her own house, which is the most romantic place anyone could step into, a personal creation. It is art without the cute. Her unfailing eye retrieves pieces old and new to be used as they are or painted the perfect color for the corner to which they're destined.

For all its artistic perfection, the house is lived in and used. For years it was the hub of teen activities for the five Burnham children and their friends. With dogs and boots and books and Anne at her drawings or coaching Latin or helping with an English paper, it was home in its totality. It was this house, not the automobile, which was the base of family life. Children walked or biked to the library, school, or athletic events.

No wonder, then, that Anne could not turn over the maintenance of the grounds to a crew of men with mowers and hedge clippers; no wonder that we met for these reviews. Anne is the artist and I the one to apply the brush to execute the unstudied effect she seeks: a nineteenth-century atmosphere in keeping with the 1840s house. Anne is too sophisticated in her tastes to fall for the prevailing country club slick, but the line between romantic and neglected is very fine, and it took more time for us to maintain this seemingly disheveled property than to manicure for a compulsively neat client.

This spring morning the lawn, which had never seen fertilizer or herbicide, was a medieval tapestry of wildflowers: in the sun, English daisies, veronica, violets, and spring beauties; under the old trees where grass couldn't grow, moss had taken over, enticing barefoot children or fairy dances. Mowing was deferred until the flowers had passed, so the grass was shaggy, and friends had been given the opportunity to dig up the buckeye seedlings (Aesculus glabra, not to be confused with the horse chestnut, Aesculus hippocastanum) that came up every spring thanks to the squirrels.

The brick house built in 1843 sat behind the trees in simple elegance. The central Greek Revival door was flanked on each side by two long windows. Anne, even as she greeted me now in blue jeans and a vivid blouse, matched the elegance of the house. She wore her hair pulled into a bun, which emphasized the high cheekbones and her classic beauty. I followed her down the stone path, stones barely showing through their cover of grass, to the street where we could have a better view of the plantings and assess the volunteers that had now reached a size to require some decisions.

A protective tangle of trees and shrubs, planted and volunteers, surrounded the grounds. The gravel drive at the side softened by a grass median was barely visible through the arch of lilacs, so the drive itself was mysterious and set the tone for the surprises to follow, for everything here was subtle.

When new gravel was needed, boards were laid over the grassy center so that the country-lane feeling would not be destroyed. It was this attention to detail that made the property so magical and serene.

Anne has a vision and a sensitivity to the spirit of place. The grounds have evolved and continue to do so. No huge out-of-context crocus had been planted for spring color (as if spring didn't have color); the miraculous millefleur turf had planted and perpetuated itself. Although it was one of the most interesting houses in town, both historically and architecturally, there had been no attempt to return it to its original state, no tearing out or uprooting for the sake of authenticity. The spirit of former generations remained.

We commented on the magnificent buckeye towering over the house. Its health was of concern, as it had suffered greatly in the last drought. It had been planted by the builder of the house, Nathan Perkins Seymour. We knew this because Anne had read all the Seymour letters written to his father in Connecticut discussing the details of the building of the house, the planting of the grounds, and even this tree. Through these letters she had a complete history of the building processes. She knew where the bricks had been made, what wood was used and where, the varieties of apples available, and the final selection and Seymour's general knowledge of plants. As with Jefferson and Washington, these intellectuals of early Hudson did not separate themselves from the natural world. Anne respected this and maintained a continuity of ideals. With the same respect, she showed me the diseased crab that was all that remained of a formal garden installed years before the house came to the Burnham family.

"I suppose it should come down," she said looking at me for some sort of confirmation, "but it is all that is left of a really beautiful formal garden." She pointed to the humps in the grass where topiaried trees had stood. "Look," she held a branch, "it has buds. In a few weeks it'll bloom, even these few branches."

"It has another year then," I said. No tree euthanasia here where age was allowed its imperfections.

"I think it so sad that people want everything perfect. It is like living in a community where no old people are allowed, just the young and beautiful," Anne commented.

"Now what about the entrance path?" This was a recurring subject. Nancy, through years of tending the property, had acquired tremendous sympathy for Anne's goals. Only the walk bothered her. "You know how Nancy wants to get at those stones and clean them up," I said. Anne, with her care to preserve a sense of time, was reluctant to fully expose the sod-covered flags, laid when the buckeye was planted. Sanitized stones would never blend with the grassy drive and weathered front door.

Now she laughed, "Why don't we say that that will be her reward after the tidying has been done. But tell her not too much, just a glimpse."

Tidying here was maintenance done with the utmost care. Dead limbs were removed, certain weeds pulled, others left where they had the right effect, like a wisp of Queen Anne's lace at the base of a tree. The myrtle was rescued where it had been ruthlessly invaded and various vines were either removed or pruned or twined into trees. It took time, as every cut required thought. Shrubs that overhung the drive were not to be cut back until the cars showed scars. This meant that it was permissible for them to hang low after a rain—after all, they would spring back in a few days. It was a garden Gertrude Jekyll or the contemporary English designer John Brookes would have approved of, both of whom like a garden to be a bit "over the top." Everyone who worked at Burnham's developed a new perspective that was held as a measure for other jobs.

This morning we discussed, along with poison ivy eradication, the volunteers that had come into the euonymous bed across the front. There were a few cherries, which we both decided could go, and to the right a locust had come in and was already seven feet. To my mind it didn't belong, but we walked across the street to visualize the mature tree and its effect on the house.

"I guess you're right. I hate to take it out, but it really is interfering with the dogwood even now, and it will block too much of the house later."

Then Anne looked down the street. The brick house stood alone, separated from an Academy dormitory by a wooded lot. "I'm afraid they will eventually put curbs in here," she lamented. "There seems to be a craving for curbs, but it's so destructive to the village atmosphere. And, after all, these streets have had perfect drainage for a hundred years. They don't need curbs."

It was a point I was to remark on ever after. Whenever I find myself in a town that has a strong presence of the nineteenth century, I realize it is mainly because of the wonderful missing edge between street and tree lawn. Here in Ohio, I think immediately of Zoar and the village of Mesopotamia where this modern hard edge has been avoided. The fashionable Niagara-on-the-Lake, touted as the best-preserved nineteenth-century town in North America, I'm sure has the money for these "improvements" but has chosen not to ruin a good thing.

We turned back to the front yard. On the opposite side of the locust we saw another special volunteer—a buckeye (Aesculus glabra) offspring of the original Seymour tree. It had come in front of a P.G. hydrangea which we had hoped would eventually blouse out toward the street.

"We can't sacrifice the buckeye," I said, "but they can't survive the way they are, and the buckeye will never tolerate transplanting. The tap root is too deep. We can transplant the hydrangea, which is still small enough to move and give the buckeye all the space and importance it needs."

We walked toward the rear to note poison ivy patches (to be removed) and the wild geranium (to be saved). A rampant multiflora rose had taken over an old crab and was all but killing it. We decided to allow some sprays to intertwine with the crab and remove the superfluous branches.

I told Anne of the fragrant arbor of multiflora rose that I had seen in one of the most sophisticated gardens in the world, that of Mien Ruys at Dedemsvaart, Holland. Anne was not surprised that it

should be cherished by a landscape architect of international fame. It seemed natural to her that a plant should be selected on its own merits, not for its rarity; nor should it be banned for commonness.

Near the back door was a wildflower garden in dense shade that was making a comeback now that the lawn rakers were not taking the leaves away from it every year. I had advised that not only should it not be raked but that composted leaves be added. Already, after two years, the trilliums and scillas and May apples had decided to thrive and multiply. The chipmunks, too. They scurried away now, tails stiff, to vanish into a hole. They ate what they pleased in this Garden of Eden, safe from persecution. The leaves from the rest of the property, which had once been carried off, were now composting to be spread for nourishment in other areas.

Now we had to decide on new plantings, fillers, and replacements. Along one very shaded border I recommended arrowwood viburnum. Toward the rear, which received more sun, old-fashioned spirea and serviceberry were to be planted. These same selections would replace empty spots in the front. The replacements were never to be too many at any one time: a few each year, almost as if nature had taken over on her own. At various times we planted sumac, witch hazel, Virginia sweetspire, all native plants with good form, flower, or berries and foliage.

I promised Anne that in the autumn we'd tackle the poison ivy on the house by cutting the stems, and maybe we could find someone brave enough to pull it down. The old brick walls were a tangle of ivies, and the myth of them harming bricks was exploded here. Anne told me that the only place that the bricks had needed repointing was where the ivy had not grown. I remembered the buildings in Europe that have been host to ivy for centuries with no ill effect.

"The birds in here in the summer are incredible." Anne said. "If you clap your hands they fly out in a cloud. In winter it's a bird apartment house and the chattering wakes us in the morning. We had a squirrel," she went on, "that built its nest between the window and the storm and raised its family as if it were in a scientist's observation box. The funny thing was that the squirrel seemed to be as interested in us as we were in it."

By the time we had made the rounds, I felt as if I had been on a retreat. There had been no rush, no interrupting telephone calls from the portable phone, no panic about rushing off somewhere to be busy, no fears about what might be destroyed by malicious creatures. There was no elaborate key system to enter the house and no entering through the garage. The front door, on this mild morning, stood wide open, inviting entry into the wide hall papered with bouquets of flamboyant hollyhocks against a tomato-red background. The exuberance of the wallpaper flowers and the hydrangea-patterned lace curtains of the huge windows, repeated the unrestrained plants outside, pushing and climbing into each other.

There at the edge in the woods the forsythia was a fountain of yellow and the spirea, allowed its full shape, would become a June bridal veil.

I walked home still under the spell of this garden—this Secret Garden. In today's blatant world the key to unlock its subtleties is all but lost, and a key is needed as surely as if it were walled. Respect for history and nature, appreciation for small things, details of plant and animal life are the keys to appreciation of a garden without one flower bed, where nothing is cultivated, everything cherished.

ALL MY PHLOX

# CHAPTER 11

# *Forced*

IT HAD STARTED SIX MONTHS before. The previous spring we had redone a perennial bed for Emily Campino in Canton—really re-done it. Lifted every plant, dug in manure and compost, replanted selectively, and added new plants and summer annuals. In September I'd gone down for an evaluation. This is the follow-through I think most gardens need, and it gives me a chance to work with the client on changes.

This evaluation had gone well. We were both satisfied with the new garden. The loosestrife had bloomed on and on; the catmint in the front among fairy roses had been a surprise to Emily, who had never seen it and appreciated not only the lavender-like blooms but the aromatic qualities; the daisies had been controlled; the rosy-headed sedum had filled in several gaps and was at its peak; the veronica, salvia, campanula had all thrived; and now the 'Blue Pearls' petunias were spilling out of the border.

Emily's antique wire bench looked perfect set on the old bricks in the niche we had created for it, surrounded by nodding cosmos; she had the romantic atmosphere she loved.

Since the spring overhaul the garden house had been moved to a new site backed up to the shrub border where the lawn sloped away on one side. Emily complained that it looked bare. I agreed. Any bed here would mainly be viewed from the porch and would need strong plants in order not to be lost. I suggested white mugwort for late bloom; on the down side, where the soil tended to be damp, meadow-sweet would give a soft look, as would maiden grass; perhaps sev-eral Russian sage; and, to complete the planting, gaura, a Bill Hen-dricks recommendation, and fountain grass. The grasses would offer winter interest, and the whole, I thought, would be soft and informal, which Emily so wanted. I would send written suggestions and plant descriptions after further consideration of the problem, but I found that my first instincts were usually correct. It was a little like sizing someone up after the first handshake.

We walked over to the herb garden, which had been more than successful, and I gave my usual scolding about cutting herbs, eating them, or drying them but not allowing them to spend the summer unrestrained.

In the course of inspecting the garden, I heard about her son's wedding planned for the following spring. Emily was always in high gear and spoke as if her words were trying to catch up with her thoughts. Now, in telling of plans for the wedding next April, she was almost panting. "With a boy there isn't much we can do, so we are going to have a big reception here the week before, just for the family. You know, with Tony's side there are so many, and all the cousins . . . and then there is my side, and we have quite a few, and what with this being our first wedding, and it being Mike instead of one of the girls, and not being able to put on the wedding I just had to do something. Come on in and I'll show you what I'm thinking."

It was a large brick house that the Campinos had built on a very spacious lot. Emily had enough energy for ten people, and what she hadn't put into her children she had put into antique collecting and decorating. She and her husband, Tony, had conflicting tastes, so to eliminate bickering they had agreed on two decors, which was quite startling unless the reason was explained. The foyer, spattered with gilt half-crescent tables holding enormous vases of silk flowers, was floored in black and white marble tiles; the living room, done in pink satin upholstery, could be seen on one side and on the other the dining room, a sort of American Louis XIV with stiff chairs, silver urns, pink brocade curtains and tassels. Passing through to the rest of the house the floor changed from marble, polished oak, and Kirman carpets to wide random boards and hooked rugs. A huge kitchen, family room, sun porch, screened porch, and back hall with bathroom were all done in "country." After all. Emily needed a place to display her finds, and through the years she had bought some gems of Ohio farm pieces: cherry tables, cupboards, settles, bowls, pottery, rugs, and anything else she could find at a good price. For her, part of the excitement was getting a bargain. She complained that the fun had gone out of collecting now that prices were so high. I wondered if the fun had gone because she was overstocked and it was hard to find something she didn't already have.

As I looked around the house I couldn't imagine what preparations were needed to get ready for a wedding or any other affair. Everything was perfect. Not a cup left on the counter, not a used towel in the bathroom, not a paper or magazine thrown casually near a chair or left on the kitchen table, and certainly no fingerprints or dog hairs anywhere. Of course, in Tony's half you wouldn't expect to see even a pillow creased; but here in Emily's big kitchen maybe a little disorder would add authenticity.

I added the lacking touch by accepting a cup of coffee and emptying my briefcase of catalogs and notebooks onto the harvest table. I was determined to get on with the garden business before Emily got on with the wedding. I knew that later she wouldn't take time to look anything up even after I had sent the written assessments. I showed her pictures of the plants I had mentioned and tried to keep her from thumbing through on her own to point out others, like delphinium, that she wanted. (I advise against these English beauties unless it is for someone who is a devoted gardener and wants to take the time to manure and water and stake and spray, as they don't take our summers of heat and humidity. With one exception: Delphinium Connecticut Yankees. I had one for about four years and for my devotion of mulching with horse manure at least three times during the season and never letting it dry out it rewarded me with masses of blue spires, which, if dead-headed, come on all summer. But how many people want to do that?) I lost my advantage with Emily when I pulled out the bulb catalogs. The garden was forgotten and the wedding was on.

"I was thinking of lots of bulbs for the reception," she said, going directly to a magazine at the note pad–telephone corner of the kitchen. "Now what I would like is something like this—you know, not looking as if it came from the florist." The *Country Home* fell open to pages for spring decor that were a combination of Ralph Lauren and Smith and Hawken. Softly lit rooms filled with mellow wood and fabrics. Perfect bulbs were artfully displayed in a variety of pots and baskets, and through open windows there was the vague background of a flowering fruit tree or a meadow of daffodils. Scilla bulged from grapevine baskets; a centerpiece of what had to be viridiflora tulips, looking as if they had been taken from a Dutch still life, arched gracefully from a celadon vase. Lily-of-the-valley bloomed in a hollowed log, and the floor under a casement window was massed with fluted terra-cotta pots of varying sizes filled with blue pansies.

"Gorgeous," I said. "How will you do it? I mean do you know a good florist who will be willing to give you more than cut flowers?"

"I was wondering if you could do something like this?"

My God! Was she serious? I laughed but bent closer over the photos. "Do you know how difficult it would be to have all these things blooming at the same time and for the one day that you have chosen? I mean, look," I pointed, "these tulips don't bloom at the same time as scilla or lily-of-the-valley." It was the typical advertising trap. "They aren't even selling bulbs; it's an ad for country curtains." I was triumphant. That was an end to it.

"Oh, I know. Clever. It certainly caught my eye. But I never had in mind this exact thing. I only showed this to give you an idea of what I had in mind. You could use what you want. Just this look is all."

She opened the doors of the big cherry cupboard and pulled out baskets, vases, pumpkin bowls, spatter ware, copper, and terra-cotta more beautiful than anything in the magazine. As she set each on the long table I saw them bursting with spring bulbs as surely as if I were looking at the real thing. Pansies, blue or blue and white, filled an old cheese tub, grape hyacinths surrounded the red tulip Praestans Fusilier in a copper wash kettle; the shape of the Ohio pottery bowl would be perfect for a mass of iris reticulata purple, and why not add Joyce in sky blue and J. S. Dyte in reddish purple? That large basket would be wonderful filled with astilbe, which I knew from the flower shows forced quite easily. "I'll have to consider the color," I was so filled with my visual fantasies I thought aloud.

Emily followed me around the room as I placed one container after the other where it might look best. She caught the spirit instantly and carried a large basket out into the hall. For the next half hour the two of us were like little girls playing house. At least I was playing; Emily was serious. With a shout I hit Tony's formal dining room. "Ah," I said pointing to the silver tureen on the side board, "perfect for angelique. She is just the pink for this room. Would you like her surrounded by white lily-of-the-valley or maybe white grape hyacinths?"

"Well then, you'll help me?" Emily bubbled. "I can hardly wait to tell the girls."

"Now wait." I woke up. What on earth was I doing? This was no joke. She really thought I would take it on. "You know," I said, "I've never forced anything in my life. I couldn't even get my children to school on time. I'll give you a call in a few days. Let me think it over."

"Oh, I knew you would be just the person to give us the look we want. It will be perfect. Let me know what I can do to help."

That had been last fall. Now it was April, and here Helen and I were, the night before Emily's reception, unloading the order from Rhonda's into the kitchen. "Why do you get yourself into this stuff?" Helen asked. Then, not waiting for an answer, "Where does this one go? It looks full out and there isn't any more room in the cool section."

"I think we can go to the back porch. After all, it is April and they only need slight protection."

Helen had come with me that day to Rhonda's for the pickup. It was a late spring and we had driven down in a cold drizzle. My worry over this project had been almost constant from the first order to the bulb companies, even with Lynna's backing, experience, and offer of space and with Rhonda's work as monitor in the greenhouse. The development of these pots of bulbs and perennials had been charted like the heartbeat of a premature baby. But the flash bulletins had done nothing to ease my mind. There was the panic call from Rhonda after Christmas to tell me that a whole batch of violas had been lost. Lynna couldn't understand why the iris, the easiest to force, hadn't even started to show. Apparently a mouse in her basement had done in some of the species tulips, and so it had gone. I became irritable and snapped at everyone. My recurring nightmare was of setting out all the beautiful containers filled with bulbs nestled cozily under their earth cover with no show of life.

Finally the last vessel was hauled in. It was the top half of a cast-iron urn filled with pink and white astilbe. I had thought that the urn would be perfect for Tony's foyer and that the plants would look more settled in if they were grown right in it, so Rhonda had done all that in her greenhouse, but we had to move the thing—cast-iron plus soil and plants. Now at last I could breathe. I had to admit that even with the losses, which no one would know about, it all looked spectacular. Some bulbs were not full out (I was counting on the overheated house to bring them on), but even the tight buds tinged with color were beautiful.

"Good old Mom. You pulled it off," Helen said, dropping her wet jacket on the floor. "It's too bad we didn't plan a party. We'll never have this again." She looked around the kitchen transformed by color and fragrance. The floor, counters, and table bloomed as if they had been touched by a fairy wand. "Anyway, I'll take a picture. No one would believe it. While I get my camera, you just sit down here with a glass of wine." I gladly did as I was told. It was the first time that I had been able to breathe easy all winter. And everything for the transportation tomorrow was ready. The banana and apple packing boxes from the grocery were all assembled in the garage; the plants from Lynna's basement were here; the sphagnum moss was bagged, as were extra pebbles and even a carpet of grass sown in cookie sheets that we had lived with for weeks on the kitchen counter. Helen took some memorable shots of a kitchen we would never see the likes of again, and I slept easy knowing that the next day's delivery would be made in the new Toyota van I had so agonized about buying, and the nightmare would end.

Next morning when I awoke I sensed, even in bed, an unnatural silence. I looked out the window. The world was muffled in a deep blanket of wet snow; one of those late freaks we can have here in northeastern Ohio. Huge flakes drifted down lazily as if they had every right to smother the tentative efforts of spring and revive my panic.

I made tea and tried to be calm. Helen came down as I was going over my options and burning toast in that stupid toaster that didn't pop up.

"Did you ever think that maybe they don't have any snow there so far south; or, if they do, that maybe they'll postpone the party?"

"No." I was sunk in gloom. I had been too optimistic last night

ALL MY PHLOX

and this was punishment for the audacity to think that I had solved the problems, that the worries were over, that life could ever run smoothly. I hated driving on winter roads, and without listening to the road report I knew that this was one of those storms that paralyzes modern society.

"I don't see why you don't phone?" Helen said logically.

"How can I phone?" I snapped. "I've promised to do a job and of course they are expecting it done. No, I'll just load up and get on with it before any more snow comes down."

"For Christ's sake! You're not the pony express. They won't expect you to come all the way from Hudson on a day like this."

"Instead of arguing you could help me load." Helen recognized the tone of voice and went to fetch the boxes from the garage. In grim silence we loaded the van, cast-iron urn and all, and I set out. The van was new and I had never driven it in snow. The first hundred yards down my own street told me all I needed to know about what to expect for the rest of the drive. The van had no traction. Tensed over the wheel, I longed for the old front-wheel-drive Honda that never faltered. I carried on.

Why did I think last night that this nightmare job was over? Except that I had heat and windshield wipers, the trip was like some I remembered as a child when my father would hang his head out the window in order to see, and my job was to hold my hand on the windshield to melt the ice.

I crept, geared down and up, spun the tires, but never actually stalled. I waited at the top of hills to make sure the road was clear so that I could make a run up the next, knowing that if I stopped it would be forever. This was a drive I usually looked forward to, through rolling Ohio farmland and one or two quiet villages, and at this time of year the yellow willows would announce that indeed, as the poet says, "spring's first green is golden"—after all, it was April. Today I saw nothing but the few feet in front of me. Visibility was a white dizzying blur. The force of the wind was from the west, and I was driving south, so across these roads the unnaturally large snowflakes fell like a road block of pernicious foam.

After hours, wound tight as a fiddle string, I arrived at the turnoff into the Campino's subdivision. My neck ached, my eyes watered from staring into the dizzying blizzard, but here I was still in one piece. A certain exultation seeped into my consciousness. I had done it. The car clock showed ten past noon. Well, a forty-minute trip had turned into three hours. As with everything to do with this job, I was not to exult too soon. The roads in this development had not been plowed. There were a few tracks to mark where the brave had ventured out and to open the way for me to venture in. No way was anything going to stop me now—not after all I had gone through. I revved the van to pull through the snow, kept grimly to

110

ALL MY PHLOX

the tracks, made the final turn, and saw the Campino's house at last, beautiful as a Christmas card scene behind the snow-laden trees. In a Currier and Ives a horse and sleigh would be cheerfully mounting the lane, the driver waving to those standing on the porch. In this reality not a mark disturbed the deep, soft, wet depths of snow on the long sloping rise of the Campino drive.

I parked in the street not daring to move out of my tracks, and slogged on foot to the front door. I had to ring several times before Emily opened, looking beautiful, makeup intact, in a housecoat of purple velvet. The sight of her looking as if she had nothing to do but to look beautiful broke me as the drive hadn't.

"The plants are down there in the car," I sobbed, "and I don't know how to get them up here or how I got here or even why."

"It's you!" She was amazed. "We never expected you today. Tony," she called over her shoulder, "it's Valerie with all the flowers. You have to shovel the walk. Mike," she called upstairs. "Get on down and help. This whole thing is for you, you know. Men!" she said knowingly. "Now just come on in and let them do something," she soothed. There was nothing I was readier to do.

Tony appeared in fushia and jade jogging togs not looking very pleased to see me if it meant going out to shovel. The boys came from nowhere to help and the car was brought to the door and unloaded while Emily made me fresh coffee. What I really needed was a stiff drink and told her so. Before pouring the coffee she added a generous tot of brandy.

"This will fix you up," she winked. She told me how lucky it was that they had planned the party for six in the evening. "What with Tony's Mom having such a time since her fall and Joanie coming over from her apartment in Cleveland, and then getting the cousins lined up, it will take most of the afternoon to get them all here. Just as well the men had to get out and shovel the drive; it had to be done sometime. They never think."

Two hours later, the house was decorated to match any magazine. The cast-iron urn now placed on its pedestal in the black and white hall got even Tony's approval. The pink of the Angelique tulips was perfect, and all the other bulbs looked as if they had been grown in their respective baskets and boxes and pottery. The turf coverings tucked around the bulbs were so fresh—especially on a day when there was no grass to be seen outside—I almost forgave the snow for what it had put me through.

By the time the last Minnow daffodils were settled into their baskets, the snow had stopped and I was ready for the drive home.

"Don't forget to send me a bill," Emily said as I left. "We won't discuss price with Tony. He thinks everything is too expensive. Drive carefully." She waved cheerfully.

How on earth do I send a bill for this one? What could it possibly be worth? All the way home, more relaxed now that the road crews had had time to plow and it had stopped snowing and the whole ghastly episode was over, I couldn't help thinking that it had been worth all the agony, even if I were never paid a cent. I had learned never to force—anything.

ALL MY PHLOX

# CHAPTER 12

# *Back to Ohio*

I<small>T'S</small> M<small>AY</small>. A lot has happened since my first plea for help years ago. Kristine and Nancy have new lives, as do the other helpers who always turned up at the right time and worked without stint. Increasingly through the years I felt frustrated at not having the time to enjoy spring, especially in my own yard. The day I returned exhausted to look out at the iris in full bloom and the gravel paths a sea of blue forget-me-nots, I burst into tears. I had been so involved with others' gardens I hadn't even had time to see what was going on in my own. It was like missing the formative years of one's own child: all the new growth, tentative shoots, swelling buds, pushy weeds, foraging insects, and sex-crazed toads had come along while I was too busy to notice. That same evening I wandered the garden in renewed wonder. The water lilies had spiraled from the bottom of the pond like green coil springs to unfold into new frog rafts.  The toads were in their orgies, the soil smelled pungent with the compost laid on last winter, and the old Hall's honeysuckle at the back door was vining and ready to bloom. This is when I love the garden most—when it is just beginning, when there is still promise, before the talents or weaknesses of the plants have been revealed, and, most especially, before I am forced to make the decisions as to who shall live with me and who shall not. One Queen Anne's lace in the far corner among the Echinacea would be beautiful, but not that whole colony. The violets, lovely as they are now, will not survive later heat, nor will the forget-me-nots. What on earth shall I do about the nigella that has drifted into one gravel path enough to block it?

After this lesson in priorities, and toting up the vigorous years left to me, even with the best of health, it wasn't hard to say yes to

George when, the following spring, he suggested we spend May in England, where the poet Browning tells us we should be.

On past visits spent admiring the profusion of English gardens, I have returned swearing never to garden again. It is too much, all those six-foot delphiniums, roses scrambling over walls and smothering cottages, the whole country garden perfectly sweet and mellow, and the climate moderate with gentle drizzles to keep lawns green and flowers fresh. What could I ever do here in Ohio? Give up, that's what!

But somehow I never did.

After this recent spring visit to England, I returned with a different attitude. I had finally come to terms with what we have and the realization that what we have is not so bad. Forget the delphiniums. The foxglove and lupins are miserable compared to those English beauties, so scratch them too. If ever a client wants hydrangeas, I'll tell them to go to the Cotswolds and enjoy them there; we can't compete, nor should we. It would be comparable to the English creating a prairie after a visit here.

But this appreciation of our own common vegetation came only after the inevitable spell that England casts on me, not to be broken until I saw the "New World" below me on the flight home.

The freshness of English spring, the exotic ragged-robin and bluebells brightening roadsides and woodlands, early roses already in bloom, stone walls transformed into trailing rock gardens—how could I not fall for the beauty of English gardens and garden landscape? I could well have been in the land of the lotus eaters, for all the will I could muster to think positively about gardening in Ohio. My new resolutions withered. All I could remember was the harsh climate. How could anyone expect to garden in a place where the temperature can fall or rise forty degrees in a few hours, where there's suffocating heat and breath-catching cold?

In England we enjoyed tea with with friends on the terrace of their fifteenth-century cottage. It was one of those English experiences where any one pleasure would have been enough—just tea on the terrace. We need not have had the homemade scones and blackcurrant jam. The terrace didn't have to be overhung with fragrant honeysuckle, and the roses on the creamy stone walls did not have to be in bloom and fragrant. To top it off, a view fell away to hedged pastures that, of course being England, held new lambs.

We walked through flowery meadows and bluebell glades and high prehistoric footpaths. We visited renowned gardens as diverse as Rosemary Verey's garden at Barnsley and the historic acres at Stourhead with vistas, grottos, lakes, and temples—where again I was making unfair comparisons.

Where, I wondered, would I take English friends visiting Ohio for anything that could compare, forgetting that I had served tea to English friends on my terrace with just such raves as I had given in England. They had thrilled at the bird life, the fragrance, the tomatoes and cucumbers picked and eaten in the hot sun.

Reliving all this on the return flight, a few imperfections in the perfection of England seeped into my consciousness: cocktails enjoyed while sitting outside in the late-afternoon sun hunched into our woolens against a very cool wind (outside because it was such a lovely day); visits to the glass house where we were told tomatoes and cucumbers grew (the only way for them to ripen); to say nothing of the endless complaints of snails not only eating the garden but marching right into the house; the gardener's dirge of acid or akaline soil or cold wet wind; fruit, even pears, netted against birds (let me tell that to goose haters at home). So, the English have problems as well.

The landscape we admire so much in Europe and England has for centuries been tended—more than merely controlled—by hand. The villages, bridges, streams, walls, meadows we love to see have evolved through years of careful shaping with what we consider today outmoded tools. The historic hedgerows of England have retained wild flora dating from the first enclosures, but even there they are being eradicated in favor of larger fields, though fortunately not without protest.

But I hear no protest when Ohio fields and woodlands are scourged by the ruthless machines we see everywhere tearing at the fabric of nature, eliminating everything—trees, undergrowth, wildflowers, the soil itself—in an arrogant effort to remake nature to our modern generic aesthetic. And does this sterility give us in the end the serenity we so much need in an ever-hectic life? No matter how many years pass for maturing, the raw scars we see replanted with a few twiggy uncomfortable imported plants can never replace the

ecosystem of molds, insects, understory, and seedlings, and certainly parking lots do not provide rest for the mind, body, or soul.

In the most romantic gardens we visited in England and Ireland the lawns were carpeted with daisies and wildflowers; in Holland, where there is little left of the wild, brush tangles are planted near apartment blocks so that children may have a "wild" place to play. But here at home the fashion is to eliminate all that is wild and replace it with landscaping-by-numbers. We have become so chemically dependent as to lose our individuality and spirit of place. If set down in St. Louis or Cleveland, we could not recognize which city we were in by the landscape. We would see no indiginous weeds or shrubs or even trees. Tourists find uneven cobbles and worn steps picturesque in Europe but will not tolerate such reminders of age here. In Hudson, for instance, the old sandstone sidewalks cannot be ripped out fast enough, even though these same Hudsonites may be among the thousands of visitors who maneuver Nantucket's quaint ankle-twisting streets.

Why do we not appreciate what is ours, what we see around us? It's time to adopt a new aesthetic for a new millenium and a punished planet. An aesthetic that would value a millefleur lawn, ragged edges, stray weeds, unmown grass, and natural growth left in place; an aesthetic tied to the rights of all the creatures we are lucky enough to cohabit with; an aesthetic tied to the health of the planet, not personal phobias against dandelions and all the multitude of creatures we consider pests.

As we came over the New World, Labrador, on this flight, I saw from thirty thousand feet what the earliest explorers must have experienced from a different perspective: vast untamed wilderness. How could I have been fickle enough to have given the English landscape my total admiration? This view was so awe inspiring, so expansive, my thoughts turned on the coureurs de bois, moose, caribou, beaver, snow fox, forests, rivers, and lakes, on all that exuberance of uncontrolled nature. And the garden that is England was left behind.

It certainly was not wilderness that I was coming home to, but it was a rambling nature, not the tidy landscape of England that's been manicured for centuries, where the glamorous swans floated on the river along with quacking ducks—staying where they should. The pastures were like lawns, not the messy tangles of my dog-walking fields; and trees were in wood lots or along hedgerows, not sprouting unbidden anywhere at all.

This year my own garden was prepared for planting. True to my new resolutions, I had played exhaustively before we left for England, taking hold of those first weeds, readying beds, even containers so that I could keep the schedule of setting out annuals by Memorial Day, when we returned. I had even made twig trellises and bean poles from branches cut from a red maple that had fallen across George's drive, made a new gate for the garden, and altogether enjoyed spring as I hadn't in years. During the flight I had mentally fine-tuned my own garden: red runner beans on the new red maple trellis installed the morning we had left. The containers, not yet planted, I saw overflowing with some new introductions from Rhonda, and the bank, I knew, was already started on its long succession of bulbs. I even took a mental walk through the fields, which by now would be fragrant with thorn apple.

So by the time the plane landed, the spell England had cast was broken. Instead of returning in frustration, I had regained appreciation for what we have, even for what are generally called nuisances: the Canada geese at the park, the chipmunks, the deer, the raccoons, all the wildlife we try to eliminate. What a privilege to see the new goslings protected by devoted parents. So what if they leave droppings behind. I've never seen a goose toss out beer cans or styrofoam cups in public places. In England wildlife is confined to parks or stocked in shooting preserves. Here we have wildlife parks in our own yards. There is hardly a morning walk that I don't see deer or fox or raccoons returning from nocturnal foraging (maybe in my own trash can). Nuisances perhaps, but, like a tree shedding leaves, worth it nonetheless. The destruction by deer can be a real menace when they overeat their own territory but not necessarily when they dine on hosta planted at the edge of "their" woods.

The unkempt fields and meadows, the hardwoods, the sumac, the cottonwoods clogging screens, multiflora rose, chicory, day lilies, thorn apple—all this messy profusion of nature is a luxury denied most Europeans who live with a controlled nature. Even our American vocabulary clings to a wildness, a roughness, we want to deny. Clients consult me about their *yard,* which has quite a different connotation from *garden.* "I want an island bed in the backyard." "I'd love to have a herb garden in the front yard." To the English the same space would be *garden,* even if it were a tangle of weeds. The English cottage garden does include the vegetables; but in Ohio I'm asked in June if I've got my "garden in," and this doesn't mean have I planted the petunias or geraniums. Rather, it asks whether I've planted the corn, beans, carrots. For many Americans *garden* remains strictly utilitarian: vegetables in rows behind the garage, perhaps shared by a few cutting flowers.

Moreover, only recently have Americans "mowed the lawn"; for generations they "cut the grass." Certainly until the prevalent use of irrigation systems it was grass that we had. This is quite different from the close lawns of England, so suited to their climate of constant drizzle and so imitated (unnatural as turf might be in many parts of the United States) and at such great expense, labor, and environmental hazard even today.

It was a glorious spring we returned to: cool so bulbs and flowering shrubs lingered, rain just when we needed it, sun warm enough to bring on the water lilies. Reports were out that frogs worldwide were in danger, but when I saw those handsome specimens ringing my ponds with their green backs and yellow fronts, clear eyes, and self-satisfied expressions, I knew that there was no problem here. At least in this little oasis there were no pesticides to poison dogs, people, insects, or amphibians. The toad spawn was already clinging to the roots of the iris (toads mate very early in spring), and the marsh marigolds were in full bloom, their reflections gilding the pond. The soil was warm enough in my microclimate to plant the beans, and the mesclun mix planted before leaving was ready for the first salad. Rhonda had some new old-heritage tomato plants she knew I would want and a new salvia that was just my style; and the balcony petunias, she assured me, had never looked so full.

"Ohio is not so bad," I said to George as we sat in the kitchen, fragrant from the lilacs that had sprung into the room when the long window was opened, creating a seasonal bouquet. "It could very well be paradise."

# List of Plants

## Mentioned in the Text

AMERICAN CRANBERRYBUSH
Viburnum trilobum

AMUR CHOKECHERRY
Prunus maacki

ARROWWOOD VIBURNUM
Viburnum dentatum

'AUTUMN JOY' SEDUM
Sedum spectabile
'Autumn Joy'

'AUTUMN LIGHT' GRASS
Miscanthus sinesis
'Autumn Light'

BALLOON FLOWER
Platycodon grandiflorum

BLACK LOCUST
Robinia pseudoacacia

BLACK-EYED SUSAN
Rudbeckia speciosa
'Goldsturm'

BLACKHAW VIBURNUM
Viburnum prunifolium

BLANKET FLOWER
Gaillardia aristata

BLUE MIST SPIREA
Caryopteris clandonensis
'Dark Knight'

BOTTLEBRUSH BUCKEYE
Aeschylus parviflora

BURKWOOD VIBURNUM
Viburnum burkwoodii

CAROLINA SILVERBELL
Halesia carolina

CASTOR PLANT
Ricinus

CATMINT
Nepeta mussinii

CHINESE DOGWOOD
Cornus kousa chinensis

CINQUEFOIL
Potentilla fragiformis

COLTSFOOT
Tussilago farfara

COMMON LILAC
Syringa vulgaris

COMMON WITCH HAZEL
Hammamelis virginiana

CORD GRASS
Spartina pectina
'Aureo-marginata'

CORN POPPY
Papaver rhoeas

CORNELIAN CHERRY

Cornus mas

CORNFLOWER

Centaurea cyanus

CREEPING JENNY

Lysimachia nummularia

'DART'S GOLDEN' NINEBARK

Physocarpus opulifolius
'Dart's Golden'

DECIDIOUS HOLLY

Ilex verticillata

DITCH LILY/DAY LILY

Hemerocallis fulva

DWARD CATTAILS

Typha minima

DWARF FALSE CYPRESS

Chamaecyparis obtusa 'Nana'

EASTERN JUNIPER

Juniperus virginiana

FLOWERING DOGWOOD

Cornus Florida

FLOWERING QUINCE

Chaenomeles speciosa

FOUNTAIN GRASS

Pennisetum alopecuroides

FRAGRANT TOBACCO PLANT

Nicotiana sylvestris

FRINGE TREE

Chionanthus virginicus

GAY FEATHER

Liatris pycnostachya

GIANT SILVER GRASS

Miscanthus floridulus

GOLDEN HINOKI FALSE CYPRESS

Chamaecyparis obtusa 'Aurea'

GOLDEN SUNBURST LOCUST

Gleditsia triacanthos inermis

'Suncole'

GRAY DOGWOOD

Cornus racemosa

HAWTHORN

Crataegus phaenopyrum

HEDGE MAPLE

Acer campestre

HELIOTROPE

Heliotropium 'Marine'

HORSE CHESTNUT

Aeschulus hippocastanum

INVASIVE LOOSESTRIFE

Lythrum salicaria

IRONWOOD

Carpinus caroliniana

JAPANESE MAPLE

Acer japonicum

JAPANESE BLOODGRASS

Imperata cylindrica 'Red
Baron'

LACEBARK PINE

Pinus bungeana

LADY'S MANTLE

Alchemilla mollis

LARKSPUR

Delphinium ajacis

LEMON LILY

Hemerocallis flava

LITTLE BLUE STEM

Andropogon scoparius

MALLOW

Malva alcea 'Fastigiata'

MANCHURIAN CHERRY

Prunus mandshurica

MANCHURIAN MAPLE

Acer manschuricum

⚓

Maiden Grass
  Miscanthus sinensis
    'Gracillima'
Marsh Marigold
  Caltha palustris
Meadow Sage
  Salvia nemerosa 'Mainacht'
Meadowsweet
  Filipendula rubra 'Venesta Alba'
Mignonette
  Reseda 'Fragrant Beauty'
Mock Orange
  Philadelphus virginalis
Mugho Pine
  Pinus mugo
Native Purple Loosestrife
  Lythrum virgatum
Nikko Maple
  Acer nikoense
Ohio Buckeye
  Aesculus glabra
Ox-eyed Daisy
  Chrysanthemum leucanthemum
P.G. Hydrangea
  Hydrangea paniculata
    'Grandiflora'
Pagoda Dogwood
  Cornus alternifolia
Partridgeberry
  Mitchella repens
Perennial Lupin
  Lupinus perennis
Pink Fleece Flower
  Polygonum reynoutria
Pokeweed
  Phytolacca americana

Purple Smoketree
  Cotinus coggygria 'Velvet
    Cloak'
Red Barberry
  Berberis thunbergii
    atropurpurea
Redosier Dogwood
  Cornus sericea
Reed Grass
  Calamagrostis acutiflora
River Birch
  Betula nigra
Russian Sage
  Perovskia atriplicifolia
Sapphireberry
  Symplocos paniculata
Scotch Pine
  Pinus sylvestris
Serviceberry
  Amelanchier canadensis
Siberian Iris
  Iris Siberica
Smallflowered Portulaca
  Portulaca umbraticola
Soapwort
  Saponaria ocymoides
Speedwell
  Veronica 'Blue Charm'
Spirea
  Spirea vanhouttei
Spurge
  Euphorbia myrsinites
Sumac
  Rhus typhina
Summersweet
  Clethra alnifolia

SWEET FERN
  Comptonia peregrina
VERNAL WITCH HAZEL
  Hamamelis vernalis
VIRGINIA SWEETSPIRE
  Itea virginica
WAND FLOWER
  Gaura lindheimeri
WEEPING BEECH
  Fagus sylvatica 'Pendula'
WEEPING WILLOWLEAF PEAR
  Pyrus salicifolia pendula
WILD BLACK-EYED SUSAN
  Rudbeckia hirta
WILD THORN APPLE
  Malus coronaria
YARROW
  Achillea
YELLOW DOGWOOD
  Cornus sericea 'Flaviramea'
YELLOW FLAG
  Iris pseudacorus
YUCCA
  Yucca filamentosa
ZEBRA GRASS
  Miscanthus sinensis 'Zebrina'